PRAISE FOR DENISE RYAN'S PINK PREP

"An essential truth that this time in history has exposed is that we can never overprepare. One simple twist of fate can be life-altering. For women – who often have to contend with a staggering amount of adversity simply because of our gender – that change can be doubly devastating. At the end of the day, I'd rather say I did too much than not enough. And if *Pink Prep* is too much, then I'm ready for it – and for the empowerment that it can help us cultivate in our daily lives."

—**LOLITA FOSTER**, Actress, *Orange is the New Black*

"My spouse and I are making sure our granddaughter is "raised ready" when disaster strikes but not every girl is so fortunate. In today's ever-changing climate many are unprepared for the challenges life can bring. At the Department of Homeland Security, we worked hard to secure the nation from the many threats we face from natural disasters to domestic threats. The more prepared each citizen is, the more prepared the country can be. Reading Denise's *Pink Prep* and implementing its recommendations can help you to be at the ready when disaster strikes."

—**DONALD R. SWAIN**, Former Department of Homeland Security Deputy Executive Secretary, Senior Executive Service and Retired Navy Medical Service Corps Officer

D1004382

"Author Denise Ryan consistently steps into the truths impacting women around the world. With a sense of humor and humility, Denise's gift throughout her career is to illuminate the possibilities for women when faced with life's most difficult challenges. It is great when you discover a valuable resource that provides crucial knowledge for women in their pursuit of a more productive and prepared life. Denise Ryan's latest book, *Pink Prep* is just that resource."

—**RENÉ STREET**, Executive Director,
American Business Women's Association

DENISE RYAN

PINK PREP

A WOMAN'S BEST GUIDE
TO PREPARING FOR THE WORST

ISBN (paperback): 978-1-7368589-0-5
ISBN (ebook): 978-1-7368589-1-2

Editor: Sandra Wendel, Write On, Inc.
Cover and Interior Design: Vanessa Mendozzi

Published by FireStar
www.PinkPrep.com
DeniseRyan@PinkPrep.com

To the prepared

CONTENTS

WHY SHOULD YOU READ THIS?

Something is headed your way. Something big and bad, and you are not ready. You don't know exactly what's coming or when it will get there, but it is coming. This book is my chance to step between the unknown peril and you.

I've seen too many strong, smart women just like you get blindsided. Maybe it was by a spouse who spent all her money. Maybe it was by COVID-19 or a car crash. If you'll take the time to read this book and follow some of the recommendations, an event that would have devastated you before will now just make you say, "Is that all you got?"

But you don't have to take me up on the offer—you can decide this isn't for you and stick your pretty little head back in the sand. Let me share some numbers first:

- Women sixty-five and older are 80 percent more likely to be impoverished than men
- 45 percent of marriages end in divorce
- 80 percent of women outlive their husbands
- 77 percent of drivers have been in at least one accident
- 41 percent of US women are obese
- 647,000 Americans die of heart disease every year
- 39.5 percent of us will have some form of cancer in our lifetimes

See? Something *is* coming. Keep reading and get ready. I'm going to turn you into a Pink Prepper.

Now don't panic. This isn't a book about growing your own food or making your own clothes. We're not building an underground bunker. This is a book about being prepared for the events most likely to mess you up and mess you up good. This book is going to help you assess your risks, then prepare you to handle them. Our mantra is Preparation = Confidence. And confidence will help you take on (and survive) anything.

Some Prepper Terms to Be Familiar With

Don't worry, dear Pink Prepper, we are not preparing for the utter breakdown of society. Armageddon isn't around the corner. But some traditional prepper terms will be helpful to know (and we'll get to sound cool when we use them).

Bug Out—Evacuate, leave in a hurry.

Bug-Out Bag—A bag full of stuff you'll need if you bug out.

Get Home Bag—If you are away from home and SHTF, this bag contains items you'll need to get back home.

Hard target—A person or place that does not look vulnerable. Evil doers pass up hard targets and look for soft ones.

Preps—Things you do to prepare.

Shelter in place—We all know this one since COVID-19. Traditional preppers take it to a different level. There will be no underground bunker discussion here.

SHTF—Shit Hits the Fan, used for disasters from massive power outages to a zombie apocalypse.

SLAE—Significant Life Altering Event.

TEOTWAWKI—The End of the World as We Know It.

WHERE DO WE START?

Weee start with COVID-19. I hope when you read this all the COVID mess is just a bad memory. I hope the millions of people rendered jobless overnight are back to work, and the businesses forced to close all made it through. I hope the kids are back in school. I hope we can shake hands and hug and go to concerts.

But as I wrote this book, my state was on lock-down (also known as sheltering at home). We didn't know how long it would last. I am healthy, with no preexisting conditions, but media reports constantly came out about young people dying or the virus mutating.

My business of twenty years (professional speaking) was shut down because people couldn't gather. Travel was restricted. Store shelves were empty in some places. We wore masks for the limited places we went, and businesses were erecting Plexiglas barriers between cashiers and customers.

When SHTF, were you ready?

Luckily, I was. I had a big fat emergency fund. I also had tons of Purell Wipes, hand sanitizer, and toilet paper—all of which you may remember were in high demand. And my beloved boyfriend, Tim, whom I had often mocked for his prepping, had thirty N95 masks. We were in high cotton.

His stockpile was a result of actual prepping; mine was due more to hoarding. But I am a financial prepper, which served me well in this unforeseen big bad event. I still don't know how long the effects of the pandemic will last (perhaps forever), but I'm profoundly grateful I was prepared. Many were not.

In the Federal Reserve's *Report of the Economic Well-Being of US Households* in 2018 (May 2019), 27 percent of households would have to borrow or sell something to cover an unforeseen expense of $400; 12 percent couldn't pay it at all. COVID-19 cost many households much more than $400.

I don't know if COVID-19 was a problem for you. Maybe you were lucky and rocked it. You were prepared to homeschool your kids, didn't lose any money, and never ran out of anything. You were able to work from home. Well done. I'd like to tell you your life will be all unicorns and rainbows from here on out, but the odds are just not in your favor.

Dear reader, I am not trying to rain on your parade. I'm trying to hand you a nice bright pink umbrella.

You Do You

Anyone who says they have all the answers for you is a liar. The only person who has the answers for you is you. My job is to provide guidance to help you be prepared for what life will throw at you. Your job is to choose what resonates with you.

You can do something as small as stocking up on hand sanitizer or as big as going back to school to earn more money. I will offer you ideas that will help you sleep at night or give you confidence. What you need to feel prepared and what I need to feel prepared could be vastly different. Your life experience, your age, your desires all play a role. I want you to live a prepared life that works for you.

You can join the Pink Prep Nation by taking responsibility for your future. You are smarter and stronger than you give yourself credit for, and you can handle anything life might throw at you—if you prepare.

STEP ONE IN PINK PREP—GET YOUR HEAD IN THE GAME

B eing a Pink Prepper is not easy. If it were, you'd already be one. You'd have a big fat emergency fund, a rock-solid prenup (prenuptial agreement), and be in excellent physical condition. But don't despair. I bet you have more prepper tendencies than you realize. You are already prepping if you do any of these:

- Stock extra supplies like batteries and toilet paper
- Have jumper cables in your car
- Have an emergency fund
- Always have some extra cash on you
- Do some form of exercise
- Carry stuff you know your kids or spouse will need but won't think of themselves

Chances are you've been planning for the unexpected without even being aware of it. Being a Pink Prepper means being strategic about your preparation and doing the heavy lifting. What do I mean by heavy lifting? Doing things that aren't fun. Things like living below your means, exercising, and having the money talk when a relationship gets serious. This book is going to tell you what to do, but if you're not mentally tough, you won't do it. But you can get tough the minute you decide to.

Jessie is Tim's daughter. She was engaged to a young man we liked, but we knew nothing about his finances. I've seen too many women (from my mother to several of my closest friends) financially devastated by their husbands. I didn't want that to happen to Jess. But I'm not her mom, I didn't raise her. And money is super emotional. I was afraid if I started asking a bunch of questions about her beloved's financial status, I would upset her (and that would upset her dad and drama would rain down upon me).

One day, Jessie said she wished she had learned more about money and finances in school. When she cracked the door, I barreled in. I said, "I'd be thrilled to teach you about money." And I led her down the Pink Prep Path to Prosperity (a path you will have the chance to walk down as well).

When Jessie (and her soon-to-be husband, Joey) started on the PP Path to Prosperity, they let me look at everything—they were financially transparent. It was an act of trust, and I was delighted to help them. (And I'm not gonna lie, I wanted to investigate Joey to make sure he wasn't a financial train wreck.)

I went through everything—ran credit reports, cross-checked account balances, logged onto employee portals—everything. And what I saw was a young couple with two decent jobs but living paycheck to paycheck.

Nothing wrong with this if life stays perfect. If they never have car trouble or a health issue. Or if they never want more, like a house they own instead of rent or a cool vacation. Living paycheck to paycheck makes you vulnerable and is not Pink Prep.

Jessie is my star pupil—she got this right away. She took them from zero savings to almost $10,000 in less than a year. If they can do this, you can too. What you need are knowledge (which I will give you) and discipline (which you have to build). Being prepared requires discipline.

3

DISCIPLINE

People who know me would say I am disciplined. I exercise at least five times a week; I save much more money than I spend; I don't waste tons of time. But I have lots of room for improvement. I love sweets; I'm addicted to true crime shows; and I have a Bath & Body Works hoarding issue. You don't have to be perfect; you have to be prepared—and that, dear reader, is going to take discipline.

After you develop your personal Pink Prep Profile, you'll know which actions you should take to live a prepared life. For some of you, it might be saving money. For others, exercising regularly. Whatever your plan is, it will require discipline. So how to become more disciplined? Here are some ideas:

Knowledge is Pink Power. You must start by knowing what to do. You can be highly disciplined, but if you are doing the wrong things, you won't get the right results. Then you'll get discouraged and give up. Let's say you want to get better at golf. You go to the driving range every day. You work hard. But if you keep practicing the same terrible swing, you won't improve. Being disciplined at doing the wrong things is a waste of time.

Discipline can spread. Being disciplined in one area of your life can spread to other areas. Start small with something easy. Maybe it's always putting items away after you use them or always making the bed or never leaving dishes in the sink. Maybe you decide to take the stairs instead of the elevator. Maybe you decide to take your lunch to work to save money. Next thing you know, you're eating healthier or working out more.

Don't wait for the perfect time—start immediately. You can have more discipline right now. Say you will read through to the end of this chapter. Better yet—read to the end of the chapter while moving or stretching. You don't have to wait to have a complete financial plan to immediately start saving. You can be a more disciplined person the moment you decide to be.

Use the power of habit. If you do something for ninety days, you own it. It's a habit. You don't have to use discipline anymore—it's who you are. Do you brush your teeth before you go to bed every night? There you go. Dental hygiene is a habit for you. You don't even think about it. Now some of you might need to add flossing. The point is, you already have a lot of habits—some serve you, some don't. I've fallen into the habit of watching Netflix every night and eating and eating—*not* serving me. I do eat the same healthy lunch every day, I don't think about it, it's habit. (You'll learn what it is in the nutrition section.) Use the power of habit to help you, not hurt you.

Do something so small it would be pathetic not to do it. Let's say your house is a mess, clutter everywhere. Instead of thinking you have to clean the entire place so it shines, simply put away one item each day. Set the goal not of walking 10,000 steps a day, but ten more steps than yesterday. I do this with email. If my inbox gets too full, I set the goal of ending each day with ten fewer email messages than the day before. You can always do more if you want, but start building a new habit by doing something so small it would be embarrassing to not do it. Consistent action in the right direction is better than sporadic huge acts you can never maintain.

Realize that little decisions lead to big screw-ups. You're trying to lose weight, and you decide to have just one chip. You're trying to stop drinking and you just pop into the bar to say hi. Those simple little decisions can open the floodgates of hell. Next thing you know, you're holding an empty family-size bag of Doritos and screaming, "The next round's on me!"

Know the main reasons people fail. One is social. If all your friends are doing it (fill in the blank—eating, drinking, shopping, not exercising), you'll want to do it too. The people we spend time with are big influences on our behavior. If all your friends tell you getting a prenup is not romantic and you should trust your future husband, then you are likely to heed their advice. Are they going to pay for your retirement when he runs off with your money and the nanny? People often want others to justify their own poor choices. You, Pink Prepper, are better than that.

Another reason people fail is emotional. They get lonely or bored or afraid. I have eaten more because I was bored than because I was hungry. Too many women let love derail them. They let their loved ones spend their money or they spend all their money on their loved ones. They would rather be broke than alone. Unfortunately, this strategy usually results in being both.

Willpower alone is often not enough. Creating an environment for success can help. It's hard to resist chocolate chip cookies in your cupboard. It's a little easier if they are two miles down the road at the grocery store. It's harder to text your ex if you've deleted all his contact info from your phone. If you can't seem to save money, have it automatically deposited into savings. Go straight to the gym after work instead of going home first. Set yourself up for success as much as possible.

Willpower can weaken if you rely on it too much. You were strong and passed on the doughnuts in the break room this morning. You toughed it out and didn't have a slice of the cele-bratory birthday cake at the office party. But when your beloved brought home ice cream? You caved and ate half a gallon. Willpower weakens over time—you can only resist so much.

Do not catastrophize. This is when you think, "Well, I missed my workout Monday, so I might as well take the week off."

Or "I overate at lunch, so I might as well pig out at dinner. I'll start over tomorrow." No! Get back on track immediately. All is not lost if you don't give up. Don't let a little slip turn into a landslide.

Learn from mistakes. When you don't do what you hoped to (don't have the discipline to act in the way you wanted to act), pay attention to what happened. Is there a friend you might need to spend less time with? Should you unsubscribe from the sale emails? Should you block that jerk you're trying to stop seeing? Experience can be an outstanding teacher.

Just start. Find yourself on the fence about exercising? Just start—tell yourself you'll only do fifteen minutes on a treadmill. I bet you'll do your whole workout. Need to tackle a big project but keep putting it off? Just start—say you'll make a list of everything involved. Getting started is the hardest part. Taking action creates momentum.

Pink Prep Principle: Discipline is doing what you need to do to reach your goals instead of what you want to do in the moment. It is the secret ingredient to make you more prepared and more successful in all areas of your life. Start small, start now, get strong.

4

EMOTIONAL TOUGHNESS

To be a Pink Prepper, you have to be emotionally strong. You must believe how you feel about yourself is more important than how others feel about you. This is true—consider all those celebrities who were adored by millions only to commit suicide. If you don't care about yourself, it doesn't matter how many others do.

You have to be strong to survive the challenges life will throw at you. It will take emotional strength to ask your beloved to be transparent about finances. It will take emotional strength to let go of friends who don't support you in reaching your goals or who constantly undermine your efforts. It will take bravery to reach out and make new friends. You have to be strong if a pandemic destroys your job or a fire sweeps through your home. Pink Prep is not for the weak.

This is not about loving other people less—it's about loving yourself as much. (I'm okay with more too. After all—the only person who will be with you every second of every day until the day you die is you. The only person you can control is you. And if you want to be able to do more for others, you better take excellent care of you.)

This is where prepping for men and prepping for women is different. Men prep for natural disasters, acts of terrorism, and zombie apocalypses. They are used to being the primary earner in the household, so are less concerned with their spouse taking their money and leaving them high and dry.

A report from UBS Wealth Management (which included surveys with nearly 1,700 married couples) found that even when women are the primary earners, 43 percent of them leave the major financial decisions to their husbands. So men don't have to worry about women taking their money—they are in charge of the money in about 85 percent of households. Men still earn more than women (for every $1 they earn, we get about 80 cents). More female parents stay at home (27%) than male parents (7%). Pregnancy impacts a woman's earning power. Read this and wake up, Pink Preppers.

The report goes on to say that 56 percent of married women leave investment and long-term financial planning decisions to their husbands, and 85 percent of these women believe their spouses know more about financial matters than they do. It's not limited to older generations. Millennial women are more likely to leave investment decisions to their husbands than any other age group.

Here's the problem: women live longer than men (average life expectancy for men is seventy-six, for women eighty-one), and the divorce rate among couples fifty and older is increasing. Eight out of ten women will end up alone and totally responsible for their finances. Jane Schwartzberg, head of client segments for UBS Wealth Management USA, said, "It's a big problem because we're not going to be prepared for what inevitably is going to come."

We are not going to be prepared for what is *inevitably* to come. Are you okay with that? I hope not, Pink Prepper. I want you to be prepared.

You don't want to have money conversations because it's not romantic? It's time to stop letting your heart run your brain. You can still love and love fiercely, but if you let your emotions make your decisions without consulting your brain, you will make some big mistakes. And those, my dear, are what I'm trying to save you from.

Apparently, a lot of women are trusting/expecting their spouses to take care of them financially forever regardless of how their lives may change. Most women don't trust their spouse to get the right items at the grocery store, but they're letting him control all the money? Have they lost their ever-loving minds? My Sleeping Beauty, you need to wake up and toughen up.

Tips for Emotional Toughness

Fly solo more. The more activities you do on your own, the stronger and more self-reliant you will be. My dad lives on a golf course and likes to sit on his back porch, drinking coffee and watching the golfers go by. In the fifteen years he has been doing this, he's never seen a woman golfing alone. He has seen lots of men golfing alone, but never a woman. What better way to work on your game than playing solo?

Traveling alone is amazing—and empowering, but I find many women won't do it. I like to travel alone because I don't have to compromise. If I want to linger at an art exhibit, I can; I don't have to worry about what someone else wants to do. It also forces me to navigate new cities and deal with new situations on my own—it makes me grow. Self-reliance is vital to Pink Prep. Try it—you might like it.

Set and enforce boundaries. Stop believing you have to be so accommodating and so nice. People with boundaries are people you respect. People with no boundaries are the world's doormats. Angela is married to Calvin whose ex-wife has some issues. One day the ex was frustrated Calvin was not calling her back, so she called Angela. She wanted Angela to get him to call her. Angela calmly said they were both adults and had to work this out themselves; she would not be the go-between. That was the last time the ex called Angela. Do not let other people's drama become your drama. Make that one of your boundaries.

Remember: you do you. If you're okay with someone showing up at your house uninvited or friending all your Facebook friends after your second date, that's fine. Everyone has different boundaries. But if those behaviors bother you, speak up. Every time you do, you will be stronger (and more respected). And every time you don't, you will be a little weaker.

Learn to say no. This is harder for most women than for men. Men don't take things as personally as we do. A man can ask another man to go for a drink, and if the second man says no, they move on. If a woman asks another woman to go for a drink, the second woman might think, "I hate to say no. I said no last time. What if she doesn't ask me again or feels I'm upset with her? Maybe I should go. But I honestly don't have time. I have to finish that report. But I don't want her to get mad at me." Then she goes and stays up half the night to finish her report.

Next time this happens, take a deep breath. If you truly don't want to go, don't go. I don't want my friends to do something with me if they don't want to, do you? If you don't want to go to the baby shower, wedding, baptism, whatever, don't go. My rule is if I can't go with joy, I'm not going.

You will get tons of requests and opportunities, and you can't say yes to all of them. Every time you say yes to something, you are saying no to something else. Your time is the most valuable asset you have, so protect it by saying no.

Face your fears. Ask yourself what scares you. Don't want to discuss money because you are afraid your beloved will leave you? If you can't be comfortable discussing something this important, that's a red flag. Let them go. Afraid if you let them go, you'll be alone forever? Please. There are almost 8 billion people on the planet—you'll find someone else. And clearly, someone better.

Being brave is not about never being afraid. It about being afraid and moving forward anyway. Every time you face a fear, you'll be stronger and more confident.

Most people are far stronger than they think they are. I know women who have beat cancer but believe they can't ask for a raise. Women who have started businesses but are afraid to ask a man out. Do something once and you own it. If you're reading this book, you lived through a global pandemic. And you're telling me you can't ask your mother-in-law to text before dropping in? You are a warrior, start acting like one.

Keep your eyes on the prize. Jessie was motivated to save because she wanted to buy a house. It's easier to tell your friends you can't go to an expensive restaurant if you have a bigger goal in mind. Do you want to have drinks or start your own business? Do you want to have a new pair of shoes or hand sanitizer and toilet paper for the next pandemic? (No one is going to see those shoes when you're sheltering in place.) Where you will be in the future depends on the plans you make and the actions you take today.

Act like a Pink Prepper. Fake it till you make it. A Pink Prepper is a strong, confident woman who knows the right lover/friend/business partner for her is the one who wants an equal, not a subordinate. A Pink Prepper takes care of herself so she won't be a burden to others. And a Pink Prepper is no one's victim. She has boundaries in place, and if people won't respect them, she finds new people.

If you act confident, people will respond to you as if you are confident, and your confidence will grow. From time to time, I get nervous before a big speech. I find if I fake it (direct eye contact, big smile, big open arm gestures, standing tall), the audience responds to me as if I am confident and, next thing I know, I am. Carry yourself like a leader, and people will treat you like a leader.

Believe in yourself. One of your greatest assets in surviving a challenge is believing you can. Preparing helps create that belief. Knowledge helps create that belief. If you believe you can't do math or you're not good at household repairs—then guess what? You're right. If you believe you can learn to do anything, you are in a much better place. And you *can* learn to do anything. You might need to put more effort in, but if all those other people can do it, so can you.

Here are some statements to give you a sense of whether you believe you can influence what happens in your life or if you think what happens has more to do with fate, luck, or other people's actions. Which statements do you agree with?

1. There is no way I can solve the problems I have.
2. If I fail at something, I need to work harder.
3. My relationship problems are caused by my partner.
4. I can choose my attitude.
5. When I succeed, it's because I was in the right place at the right time.

6. Good or bad luck can follow you.

7. What happens to me in the future mostly depends on me.

If you agree with 1, 3, 5, and 6—you tend to believe others and luck determine what happens to you. If you agree with 2, 4, and 7—you feel your actions impact what happens to you. People who believe they can influence what happens to them are much more likely to survive disasters than those who believe they have no control. If you are reading this book, you realize the person most likely to take care of you when a challenge hits—is you.

Fight your normalcy bias. We all believe tomorrow will be about the same as today. We think our spouses will behave the way they always have, the air will be breathable, our jobs will be safe, clean water will come out of the tap, and chocolate bars will be available for purchase. Pink Prepping requires you to be unbiased in this regard. It requires you to consider what things are most likely to change and be ready for them. The coronavirus was the perfect example of something outside the norm, but change doesn't have to be that dramatic.

Six months after buying a new car, I was driving in the middle of nowhere at night when the oil light came on. I had to pull over to check the owner's manual, which informed me I was dangerously low on oil and should stop driving immediately. Immediately? At night? In the middle of nowhere? Oh hell no.

So I do what any strong, independent woman would do, I called my boyfriend. He said, "Stop driving—you'll ruin the engine." I explained my situation.

He said, "Get to the nearest gas station and call back."

I was freaking out. Was I destroying my new car? It started raining.

Great. I got to the sketchiest gas station in the US, popped the hood (which took a few minutes to even figure out), and tried to check the oil in the rain in the dark. I had no idea what I was doing, no flashlight, and no raincoat, and two random men were hanging out in front of the convenience store. Luckily, this hellhole sold oil, because checking mine proved I was completely out.

Leaving home earlier that night, I had thought, "I have a new car, it won't have any problems." Did I have a flashlight in the car? No, why would I? There's a flashlight on my phone. One you can't use if you're talking to someone who's trying to tell you how to check the damn oil. And a stupid phone flashlight doesn't work for this anyway. Did I have a raincoat in the car? No. Why do I need that? I have an umbrella. Yeah. Try to hold an umbrella while checking oil in the dark and keeping an eye on two randos.

I am the walking advertisement for why women need to be Pink Preppers. So much could have gone wrong here because I was completely unprepared. I've driven at night, in the rain, in a dependable vehicle to speaking engagements for twenty years. Nothing like this has ever happened, so I thought it never would. That is normalcy bias.

- 5 -

CRITICAL THINKING

It's hard to be prepared if you can't gather and interpret information. I don't mean doing a quick Google search. We have more information at our fingertips than at any time in human history, but I swear we are less informed. You must be different; you have to be better. To truly be prepared, you must be smart.

Be a lifelong learner. I've been reading about finance and health for decades. Don't get me wrong, I read for pleasure too. Do what works for you, but to be a Pink Prepper, I recommend picking at least one of the topics we cover here (relationships, finances, health, safe travel, emergency prep) and add it to your list for lifelong study. Pick several sources of legitimate information and read them regularly. (I suggest some books at the end of this one.)

For finance, I read the *Wall Street Journal* and *Kiplinger's Personal Finance*. For health, I read newsletters from several medical schools. Get your information from reputable, dependable sources. People share posts on Facebook all the time that are false. Wikipedia is not much better. The theory behind Wikipedia is that a bunch of people working together generate better entries than one person working alone: the so-called wisdom of the crowd. If you had to have brain surgery, would you rather have one qualified surgeon operate on you or forty-three contributors to Wikipedia?

Always check your sources and use more than one. Whenever someone in our family tells me something that seems unlikely, I give them "the look" and in about three seconds prove it false. (Snopes.com is an excellent site for debunking urban legend and finding fact.) Of course, my friends and family hate when I do this, but someone has to fight for facts. My goal is to encourage them to think and not believe every arbitrary article they read online. Critical thinking is apparently becoming a lost art.

Expertise in one area does not mean expertise in all. Actors know a lot about acting. Their views on public policy? Those are their views, that's it. They have a platform, but it doesn't mean they have applicable knowledge. The same can be said for professional athletes and other celebrities. A person may have won the Nobel Prize for poetry, but that doesn't mean they know anything about economics. I'm a big fan of experts, but choose your expert wisely.

Don't follow the herd. This is a human tendency. On Amazon Prime Day, I found myself looking twice at items simply because a lot of people were buying them. Items I didn't care about at all suddenly became desirable because so many people had purchased them. If everyone is doing something, stop and ask if it's truly what you want to do. Don't be lulled into belief or complacency by apparent popularity.

Those things won't happen to me. We tend to believe bad things happen to other people. This is referred to as risk optimism. That's why 90 percent of automobile drivers think they are safer drivers than other people. Most smokers think they won't get lung cancer. Many gay men refused to wear condoms during the height of the AIDS epidemic. Some people didn't practice social distancing or wear masks during COVID-19. All thinking, "I won't get hurt/sick—that happens to other people."

Guess what? Other people is us. I bet there is a risky thing or two you've done believing, "I won't get caught/sick/hurt." By doing the work of Pink Prep, you will realize the areas in which you are being too optimistic about your risk.

Remind yourself that "if it bleeds, it leads." Ratings for The Weather Channel go up when the storm of the century is supposedly heading our way. One of my favorite YouTube clips shows a weather reporter leaning into the wind, bracing himself against the onslaught of the storm as two youths calmly stroll by in the background. Oops. Check multiple sources before panicking.

Listen to what they say on Fox and on CNN. The COVID-19 crisis taught us that the world can be viewed differently based on politics. And when something is first being reported, it's possible the organization reporting doesn't have all the facts—they are rushing to be first. News agencies have made reports based on a tweet before verifying. Let the dust settle before you react. You can do this and not panic, Pink Prepper, because you have already prepared. You are five steps ahead.

Look for hidden agendas. Hundreds of websites look like review sites, but if you dig deeper, you'll see they are actually disguised sales sites. If you are looking for health or medical information and the site is selling anything or has advertisements, look for another site. You can find dozens of negative articles about Dr. Oz online. When he sells something that will "melt pounds away," he loses credibility. That is selling magic potions to make money, not to make you healthier. Maybe a source is pushing false information not to get rich, but to further a political or other cause. Be a truth seeker.

Think for yourself. This seems easy, but when was the last time you deeply thought about something? A time when you weren't listening to music or texting or Googling or scrolling around on your phone, and you were silent and thinking. We don't think much anymore. We tend to be uncomfortable without distraction. This makes you weak.

Here are some exercises to help:

- Next time you are driving, keep the vehicle quiet (no music, audiobooks, or podcasts) and consider a challenge in your life. Generate ideas and solutions.
- Next time you have to wait, don't immediately grab your phone. Stay present and examine your surroundings. People watch for at least five minutes.
- Next time you hear something you think is baloney, do the work. Research and check if it is true. Then take it another step: consider why this information would be distributed. Money? Clicks? Politics?
- Next time you travel, remove the headphones. Engage with the world around you. I booked a speaking engagement once by chatting with my seatmate on a flight. Or use the time to think. Get inside your own head; stop relying on others to fill it up.

Keep it real. Much of what you see online is curated. I can't tell you how many people have posted sappy homages to their beloved and three weeks later broke up with them. Filters make people look younger and more attractive than they are. People exaggerate, embellish, and outright lie. Spend less time in this fantasyland and you'll be happier and smarter.

Don't fall into these traps—

- **All or nothing thinking:** I am guilty of this. If I can't do my full workout, I'll do no workout. I either put up all the Christmas decorations or no Christmas decorations. This is also black and white thinking—it makes it impossible to be flexible. When a SLAE happens, you need to be flexible. When COVID shut down meetings, I didn't want to give virtual presentations. Stupid. Don't be me.

- **Mind reading:** People do this all the time. They assume they know what's going on in someone else's head. A man told me how angry he was at people who were refusing to wear masks during COVID. He said they were all ignorant and selfish. But he doesn't know them. Maybe they have respiratory issues or left their mask at home or are simply afraid. People do this with family members all the time— assume they know their thoughts and motives. You never know what's going on in someone else's mind (even if you gave birth to them).

- **Personalizing:** Thinking that everything has something to do with you. My Mask Man was convinced everyone he saw without a mask was doing it to provoke an altercation with him. Seriously? Maybe your boss came in and didn't say good morning to you. You might immediately think, "Oh no, she's mad at me." Isn't it more likely that she had something else on her mind? We all tend to believe the world revolves around us. Sadly, it revolves around the sun.

- **Exaggerating:** Either the positive or the negative. Often, we turn a small setback into a huge deal. "Tom is leaving me; my life is over." When in truth, Tom was a self-absorbed jerk and you're lucky to be rid of him.

- **Overconfidence:** Most people are convinced they are better-than-average drivers (mathematically impossible). They believe they are less likely than others to get divorced, fired, or diagnosed with cancer. They think they look younger than others their age. They are sure they will never be victims of violence or natural disaster. They are irrational.

- **Panic:** Makes us stupid and ineffectual. There was a lot of panicking during COVID-19. People were fighting over toilet paper and other supplies. I was panicky at first about the loss of my income. The cure for panic = preparation.

Best habits for effective thinking—

- Focus on the problems you can solve, not issues clearly outside your control. Currently, I'm focusing on getting this book done, not the COVID pandemic. Unless I can develop a vaccine, there's not much I can do about it.

- Focus on one problem at a time. Otherwise, you can get paralyzed. You can only do one thing at a time (effective multitasking is a myth).

- Anything that sounds too good to be true, probably is.

- If it's important, do your own research. You'll gain knowledge, increase your confidence, and make better decisions.
- Realize your best tool for surviving life's challenges is your brain.

- 6 -

DEPENDENTS

I'm going to use the word *dependent* to mean any living thing that is dependent upon you for its survival. This ranges from houseplants to pets to children and aging parents or other family members.

Let's start with plants (I'm going to work up to the hard stuff). I love plants, I have lots of them in my home. When I leave town for extended periods, I make arrangements to have them watered. From time to time, I have to repot them. They take some of my resources, but I feel the beauty they provide is worth it. But if all hell breaks loose, I'm leaving the damn plants. I won't be dragging them out in a fire.

Let's take it up a level. We have two dogs we consider our children. We spend a ton of money on food and toys and chews and vet bills (oh, the vet bills). I always have plenty of their food on hand. If we had to evacuate, we would take them with us. But some hotels won't take dogs, so we have a plan for that. We have their care included in our wills. (No kidding. A pet sitter told us we had to have a plan in case we never came back from our vacation. Go, Pet Prepper!)

Some people abandon their pets by the side of the road because they don't want them anymore. (I believe there is a special place in hell for these people.) Pink Preppers should not bring anything living into their homes they are not willing to plan for and take care of. They will do their homework and learn what they are getting into before bringing home a cute puppy or bunny or anything else. Living things require time and money, and if you aren't willing or able to commit, do not get a pet.

However, mistakes are made and life circumstances change. If this happens, make sure you find a nice home for it. Abandoning an animal you loved is wrong and there is no excuse for it. Now, if it has health issues you cannot pay for, I am not telling you to go into debt. You have to make these decisions for yourself. What I will tell you is there is risk in getting a pet, and if you don't have an emergency fund, step away from that doggie in the window. Be responsible.

It's getting serious now, Pink Prepper. I'm going to talk about human dependents. Those amazing children you would lay down your life for. Well, here's a scary number: 45 percent of pregnancies in the US are unplanned. Unprepped. The single most important decision a person can make in her entire life and almost half of mothers aren't even making it. That is definitely not Pink Prep. Why does this happen?

According to the CDC, most unintended pregnancies result from not using contraception or from not using it consistently or correctly. In other words, use contraception correctly, and you won't have a child until you have planned to have a child. (The Pill is 99.9% effective, but you have to take it every day. This, dear prepper, is not rocket science.) You owe it to your child to have a plan for providing for it, and you owe it to your child to make sure its father is on board.

I'm not saying you have to be married, I'm not saying the baby daddy has to even be in the child's life if you don't want that. But you need to be prepared. And using someone as a sperm donor without consulting him is deceptive to say the least. Consult him and sign the legal paperwork that says he has no rights if that is what you want. Do it straight up, in the light of day and dot your i's and cross your t's. Are you taking care of this life you've decided to create or not?

I've heard that saying, "There will never be a perfect time." Mostly from relatives who want you to pop out a baby for them to play with. And I get that—every little thing doesn't have to be perfect. But you do need a plan for providing for the child and for yourself.

I recently had a conversation with a young woman who was not on the Pill. She was a student and her husband (who happened to be my stepson) was getting out of the army and would be looking for work. She said, "I'm not on the Pill, if it happens it happens. I'm okay with that."

I said, "I'm not. In a few weeks neither of you will have a job. You can't take care of yourselves, much less a baby."

She was furious. Sorry, the truth hurts. If you can't provide for yourself, you have no business having a baby. Take the damn Pill.

I just said you need to have some money in the bank before you get a dog. You absolutely need to have money saved before you have a child. Be a Pink Prepper, save some money, talk with the baby daddy about care issues and everything else, talk with yourself about the sacrifices you'll have to make and be certain you're okay with it all. Make sure you're having a child for the right reasons, not because you are lonely or want to save your marriage or get someone to stay with you.

And if this makes you think twice before having children, good. You make a list before you go to the grocery store, you should have a plan before you have a baby. Whew—okay, I'm off my soapbox.

I'm not going to talk much about dependents—animal, vegetable, or mineral—going forward. But I mention them because if you are responsible for them, you have to prep not only for you, but also for them. And you have to take care of yourself because their survival depends on your survival. It's why the airlines tell you to put your oxygen mask on first. You can't save Little Suzy if you're passed out in the aisle. And get over believing it's selfish to think of yourself first. The stronger and more prepared you are, the more you can help others.

STEP TWO IN PINK PREP–
ASSESS YOUR RISK

Millions of things *might* happen. You're going to focus on those most likely to happen to you. To help, I created a risk assessment so you can prioritize your prepping.

When assessing risk, you look at the likelihood of something happening as well as its possible impact on you. For example, it's way more likely you'll get arthritis than die in a house fire. But obviously the impact is not as great. When you put numbers to all this, you get a clearer picture of your risk profile.

Your risk assessment depends on a lot of factors—including how well you have already prepared. You might be in excellent physical condition so your risk assessment will be different from that of someone with high blood pressure. Someone who lives in Chicago has a greater chance of getting hit by a bus than someone who lives in Sturgis, South Dakota.

Some of the assessment is subjective but completing it will give you guidance on where to begin. (And you might be surprised at some of your results.)

Make sure you revisit this assessment and adjust your scores as you have major life changes. All it takes is for one of your children to marry a psychopath and your assessment changes dramatically.

Find the risk assessment grid at the back of this book. I also have a downloadable version on my website at www.PinkPrep.com.

Consider and understand the risk percentages. For example, you will see I have placed pandemic at 100 percent. Experts are certain there will be more of these, but they don't know when. So it's not a guarantee one will happen in any given year, but one will happen again. I want you to be ready (in other words, no Pink Preppers will need to fight over toilet paper or hand sanitizer ever again). Before completing the assessment, please read the notes I have for each risk to help with your scoring.

The categories I use are the most important for women: relationship, financial, health, travel, and disasters. If you want more on long-term disaster risks, there are several books listed in the back of this book. Pink Preppers are practical. They know if you don't have a healthy emergency fund, you don't need to spend your hard-earned dollars preparing for nuclear winter. With the COVID-19 pandemic, it made more sense to have lowered your blood pressure than to have trained in munitions (at least as of this writing).

Pink Preppers will complete the table, assess their risks, then start preparing for what is most likely to happen to them. Not to say a Pink Prepper can't train in munitions or build a bunker if she chooses; she's just going to do other tasks first.

Keep in mind that people aren't rational. We worry more about shark attacks than heart attacks (although heart attacks are much more likely to kill us) because shark attacks seem scarier. People drive because they are afraid of flying, but driving is much more dangerous. By working through this assessment, we are trying to be rational in preparing for what is more likely (outliving your spouse) instead of what might be more scary (nuclear war).

Likelihood for You—Assessment Scale

Assign points in column C using this scale (review my suggestions first, then you do you, never forgetting the normalcy bias):

> **Does not apply** = assign a score of zero
> **Probably not or less than 20% chance** = assign a score of 1
> **Not very likely or 20% to 40% chance** = assign a score of 2
> **May or may not happen or 41% to 60% chance** = assign a score of 3
> **Likely or 61% to 80% chance** = assign a score of 4
> **Very likely or greater than 80% chance** = assign a score of 5

After assessing the likelihood of these events, you'll assess their impact on you. Your risk score is the likelihood of an event multiplied by its impact.

Impact On You—Assessment Scale

How each of these will impact you is subjective. Some are easy—a house fire is a 5. You could lose everything, people could die. For others you'll have to use your judgment. The same event could be a 1 for one person and a 4 for another. As an example, for some people losing $25,000 isn't a big deal; for others, it's catastrophic.

Assign points in column D using this scale (review my suggestions first, then you do you, never forgetting the normalcy bias):

No impact: This won't impact you much if at all = assign a score of 1

Minor impact: Financial loss not greater than $400, no missing work, no excessive emotional or mental turmoil (for example, a traffic ticket) = assign a score of 2

Major impact: Loss of income, tremendous emotional or mental turmoil, financial loss greater than $400 up to $10,000 (for example, a hip replacement) = assign a score of 3

Hazardous: Serious injury, long-term career impact, financial loss greater than $10,000 (for example early-stage cancer diagnosis) = assign a score of 4

Catastrophic: This could kill you, destroy your home, prevent you from working ever again, total loss of assets (natural disaster, war, late-stage cancer diagnosis) = assign a score of 5

We'll take each possible event one by one. Trust me, Pink Prepper, this work may seem hard or scary, but it is empowering. Your fears will be put in perspective with facts. You'll learn how to deal with anything life can throw at you. You are Wonder Woman, and you are about to put on your golden bracelets. Preparation = Confidence.

RELATIONSHIP RISKS

DIVORCE/BREAKUP

▶ Likelihood Score

This is important to be prepared for because, as discussed earlier, women tend to be financially dependent on their spouses (or at least they let their spouses control the money, making them financially vulnerable to them).

A breakup won't kill you, but unfortunately there is a 45 percent chance it will happen. To do risk assessment right, you must assign that percentage even if you believe everything is grand. If you blithely say, "Oh, we are in total love and my sweetheart will never leave me," you are missing the entire point of this book. We must be prepared for what we do not see coming.

Hopefully, you will ride off on your unicorn into the rainbow sunset together and live happily ever after. However, I (as your fairy godmother) want to make sure if Prince Charming hooks up with Rapunzel or gets turned to ash by a dragon, you, my Pink Princess, will be okay. You might not be happy, but you will be okay. You'll be prepared to build your own damn castle.

Likelihood would be a 3—may or may not happen. If you are single, dear Pink One, it's a zero.

▶ Impact Score

If you are financially dependent on your spouse, the impact of a divorce is tremendous. If you aren't, yay! You may be single, or you may be the major breadwinner and control the money. But if you are married (or in a long-term, committed relationship), a breakup may still have a huge impact on you.

For example, Tim and I are not married, but we bought our house together. Our lives are intertwined. I'm not financially vulnerable to him, but I love him, and a breakup would be terribly painful. Dealing with the house would be challenging—someone would be moving.

If you have children, the breakup of the family will be even more hurtful and complicated. Children or other dependent family members have to be considered in your impact score. Children are four times more likely to live with their mothers after a divorce or split, so you must consider that in your calculations.

Single? Woohoo? Rate that a 1, my dear.

For the rest of you, 3 or 4.

DEATH OF PARTNER

▶ Likelihood Score

Some 80 percent of married women will outlive their partners. (For the purpose of the assessment, consider yourself married if you are in a long-term, committed relationship.) According to the CDC, women live to be eighty-one, men only seventy-six. And most women are 2.5 years younger than their husbands. So the likelihood of you experiencing the death of your partner is quite high. It is a risk for the same reasons as divorce, with the twist that you might be quite old when you're dealing with it.

I'm going to say this is a 4.5—it's likely you will outlive your spouse/partner. While these numbers are based on heterosexual marriage, if you have a same-sex spouse or partner, calculate this based on your ages and your life expectancies of eighty-one. (And if you're a cougar—go girl! Maybe this won't apply to you.)

If you are single, this is a zero. If you or your beloved have health issues, or one of you is a logger or a fisher person (apparently the most dangerous jobs in the world), the score may also change. I can't describe every possible scenario, but this provides some guidance. And if I have you considering your risk, then I have you on the right path, Little Pink One.

▶ Impact Score

Single, of course, is 1.

For everyone else, this is similar to divorce. There will be the added cost of funeral arrangements, but you might be inheriting a lot of money (or you may be left with a lot of debt). If you are elderly and completely dependent on your spouse, this is catastrophic (5) if not planned for.

ABUSE (EMOTIONAL, PHYSICAL, ANY TYPE)

▶ Likelihood Score

According to the National Coalition Against Domestic Violence, one in four women has been the victim of violence by an intimate partner. Holy smokes! It happens to men too (one in nine), but more often to women, and most often when young (eighteen to twenty-four).

Here's the Pink Prep philosophy on this: you need to be prepared for anything—and if your partner mistreats you, you need to be prepared to leave. Unacceptable is any type of physical abuse. Period. Where it gets murky is emotional abuse. We all know it when we see it happening to someone else, but when you are blinded by love, well, you may downplay it.

Here's the deal, if a person loves you, they do not put you down. They do not make you cry. They do not lie to you. They treat you with respect. If your partner is causing you a lot of emotional pain, it is time to get help or get out. Pink Preppers do not stay with people who abuse them. They are strong, independent, self-reliant women. If you are not there yet, my goal is to get you there.

In their excellent article, *Domestic Violence,* authors Martin R. Huecker and William Smock state that abusers tend to

- Drink to excess and use drugs,
- Be possessive, jealous, suspicious, and paranoid,
- Be controlling of everyday family activity including finances and social activities,
- Suffer low self-esteem,
- Be emotionally dependent—they may move too fast, talking about love and marriage far too early in the relationship.

Pay attention to any of these red flags. The sooner you end something that could go bad, the better. The longer you stay with someone who hurts you, the less of yourself you will have left. And Pink Prepper, look out for your sisters. One in four? Especially the youngest of us? Give your daughters this book, talk to them about abuse. They are too precious to be hurt by someone who is supposed to love them.

Likelihood is probably a 2 for most. It increases if you are younger and have less education. If you have a partner who already mistreats you, this is a 5. If you are single, zero.

▶ **Impact Score**

Single—off the hook again.

For the rest of you, it depends on many factors—the length of the relationship, your dependence on your partner, the severity of the abuse, your support network or lack thereof. If you are being abused, over time abuse tends to escalate. Also, according to the US Department of Health & Human Services Office on Women's Health, the longer you stay in an abusive relationship, the greater the physical and emotional toll. You might become depressed and anxious or begin to doubt your ability to take care of yourself. You might feel helpless or paralyzed. Powerless. And, at the extreme, you might be killed.

According to the CDC, US crime reports found that over half of female homicide victims were killed by a current or former male intimate partner. Many women suffering abuse don't think it's possible the jerk they are with would escalate to that level. Until he does.

This a 5. If you stay in an abusive relationship, it's going to get worse over time and could cost you your sense of self or your life. The impact is catastrophic.

RAPE

▶ Likelihood Score

Rape is a horrible act to contemplate. According to the National Sexual Violence Resource Center, 18 percent of women have been raped over their lifetimes. (It's difficult to find numbers for sexual assault because it often goes unreported, so these numbers may be low.)

About 50 percent of rapes are committed by intimate partners, another 40 percent by acquaintances and less than 10 percent by strangers. This is why I included rape in the relationship section. It is terrible, but the men most likely to rape us are men we know. Ninety percent of reported rapes were perpetrated by people the victim knew. We are most afraid of the unknown attacker, but that is a rare occurrence. The greatest risk is from those we know and when we are young (under the age of thirty-four).

Impact is huge—definitely a 5.

BETRAYAL

▶ Likelihood Score

There is a 20 percent chance your beloved will cheat on you. Clearly, they are insane, but some people are weak. I want you to have options if this occurs. Prepared = Powerful. If you already have suspicions, you might want to increase this score, otherwise, give it a 2 (single = zero). We want to be prepared.

If any of you are thinking, "Well, isn't this depressing," turn the clock back to January 2020. If I said, "Hey, we need to prepare for a global pandemic. The experts say it will happen." Do you want to be the one who said, "Geez, what a buzz kill" or the one with seventy-five rolls of toilet paper, a box of masks, and a jug of hand sanitizer? I'm protecting you from mayhem.

▶ Impact Score

Single—1.

Been going out a month and you can see he's back on Match.com? His loss. Dump him and move on—2.

Been going out a while, considering marriage? Be glad you found out now—3.

You need to have been together for more than a year and/or be married or have kids to get up to 4. And, of course, you are leaving him (or her). The best indicator of future behavior is past behavior. If this person cheated on you and lied to you once, is it worth being haunted by that for the rest of your life? Do you want to always worry if they come home late from work? Or if they seem to be checking their phone a lot? Living in a constant state of suspicion is living in hell. Don't you deserve better?

It is better to be alone than with someone who doesn't want to be with you. Score this appropriately for your situation. If you have an open relationship, go ahead, and give yourself a 1. But bump it up to 4 when you start stalking his mistress.

OTHER FAMILY CRISIS

►Likelihood Score

I include this because it's often the woman who is expected to deal with these. The crisis could be an adult child wanting to move back home, an elderly parent needing care, a substance abuse issue.

You know your relatives; you have to assess your risk here. Do your parents have the resources to care for themselves as they age? Are you going to have to pick up the tab? Do you need to have a tough conversation here, Pink Prepper? We do not stick our heads in the sand. Are you and your baby daddy/mama on the same page as far as supporting kids financially after they graduate? Are there substance abuse issues in the picture? (About 25 percent of Americans are binge drinkers, one in five has a mental illness, one in twelve has a substance abuse disorder.) Get these on your radar, assess their likelihood, and assign them a value. Other people can mess you up if you're not prepared.

Let me give you some scenarios to help you assess. If your parents are wealthy and have planned for their long-term care and you don't have children, this is a 1. If you have children with no addictions and your parents have passed away, this might be a 2. If there is addiction in your family, I'd say your score should be at least a 4. If you have an adult child who makes terrible decisions, 4. If you have aging parents who have saved little and are in poor health, at least 3.5.

►Impact Score

This depends on the crisis and how you are wired. Can you set boundaries and say no? How emotional are you? I'm a rock. For me this is probably a

2.5. But you may be a softer touch and will bankrupt yourself in an effort to help others. For you, it could be a 4 or 4.5. Watch a few episodes of *Intervention* and you'll see what I mean. Almost every episode features a parent letting their marriage, their other children, and their life savings all go up in flames as they try to "save" an addicted child. Honestly assess the impact this might have on you.

FINANCIAL RISKS

Money is a big deal for Pink Preppers. As we've discussed, women tend to earn less than men; they feel less confident in their knowledge of finance; and in the case of a divorce, they are likely to have care of the children (which takes time and money). During the COVID-19 crisis, women lost more jobs than men, and they carried the bulk of the childcare responsibilities. Reports say this will impact women financially for years to come.

You can't be prepared for much if you don't have money. And if you feel money is bad or evil, you need to get over that right now. Money is a tool—it can be used for good or for bad just like a hammer. Money can build a hospital, or it can help your spouse hire a better divorce attorney. The more you have of it, the more prepared you are. Period.

UNEXPECTED FINANCIAL LOSS

▶ **Likelihood Score**

This often accompanies another event listed here—divorce, natural disaster, pandemic. And many of us are not ready to handle it. This is from the Federal Reserve's *Report on the Economic Well-Being of US Households in 2018* (May 2019):

If faced with an unexpected expense of $400, 27 percent of adults would have to borrow or sell something to pay for the expense, and 12 percent would not be able to cover the expense at all.

Seventeen percent of adults are not able to pay all of their current month's bills in full. Another 12 percent of adults would be unable to pay their current month's bills if they also had an unexpected $400 expense that they had to pay.

One-fifth of adults had major, unexpected medical bills to pay in the prior year. One-fourth of adults skipped necessary medical care in 2018 because they were unable to afford the cost.

These numbers tell me that at least 39 percent of us are living on the edge. You are going to have unexpected expenses. There is a 100 percent chance of that. The size of the expense and its impact will vary, but you will have one. It could be an unexpectedly hot summer resulting in a big electric bill. It could be an increase in the price of groceries or a flat tire. Or it could be something huge—a job loss, a divorce, a car accident.

There were few people *in the entire world* who did not (at least initially) experience a financial loss due to COVID-19. Millions of jobs were temporarily or permanently lost; many of those still employed were asked to take pay cuts; investment portfolios lost value and on and on. And many people were not prepared.

This is a 5, my pretties.

▶ Impact Score

This has everything to do with the size of the loss. The Federal Reserve worked with $400. But I'm going to use a different measure—four weeks of your current pay. Let's say you earn $500 a week. Assess the impact based on a loss of $2,000. If your income varies, take an average.

Why am I using this measure? During the COVID-19 crisis, people lost their jobs right and left. The system to apply for unemployment in many states was malfunctioning due to the onslaught of applications. People went weeks without pay. So this is a minimum. If you lost four weeks of pay (or if your spouse supports you and he lost four weeks of pay), how much would this impact you? I'd say a 3 for most people. Remember, my impact scores are guides. For wealthy people, this might be a 1 or 2. For poorer people, it could be close to catastrophic (5).

IDENTITY THEFT

►Likelihood Score

This is my nightmare: some freak taking all my money, messing up my credit, and doing who knows what else in my name. There are horror stories about people whose identities are stolen, and they have to fight for years to get them back. Luckily, the likelihood of it happening is only 16 percent—so that's a 1. Whew.

►Impact Score

While this is not likely to happen, it would be a nightmare if it did. I'd say the impact is at least a 3.

CYBER ATTACK (RANSOMWARE, VIRUS)

►Likelihood Score

My business is almost completely on my computer—my customer database, my books and materials—years and years of work. We have all heard about cyber criminals holding someone's computer and all its files for ransom. It doesn't happen as much as you might think—23 percent chance. That's a 2.

► **Impact Score**

This depends on how important what's on your computer is to you. For me, it's a 3.

NOT HAVING ENOUGH FOR RETIREMENT

► **Likelihood Score**

Only 39 percent of women say they are confident they will have enough for retirement. I'm surprised the number is this high. Why? Because of the Pink Prepper law—if it can go wrong, it damn well might. The stock market could tank. It's done it before and will do it again. You may be healthy now, but you (or your spouse) might need to go into care in your elder years—that is crazy expensive. Even if you have long-term care insurance, there's no guarantee it will cover everything or that the company providing it won't go bankrupt.

Only 5.8 percent of US households contain millionaires, so these ladies aren't confident because they are rich. Maybe they trust social security to provide for them? Personally, I'm assuming social security might collapse by the time I retire. Even if it doesn't, it likely won't be enough.

Let's run some quick numbers. Average annual household income in the US is about $61,000 a year. If the earner(s) retire at sixty-five and live for another twenty years, they'll need about a million dollars to fund their retirement. Their expenses may go down in retirement. There may be a pension or other source of income. The women will be single for part of this time and so forth. The 39 percent (all of whom are clearly not millionaires) might be a bit optimistic. Maybe some of them believe their husbands have them covered. (The same husbands they don't trust to do the grocery shopping.)

I've got quite a bit of money saved for retirement, and I still won't say I'm confident I'll have enough. I am sticking with hopeful. There are too many variables beyond my control to let my guard down. (For example, my calculations never included over a year of income lost to a pandemic.)

Women sixty-five and older are 80 percent more likely to be impoverished than men. And 40 percent of women have no plan for their retirement. Almost one-fifth of working women have nothing saved for retirement, according to a 2020 CNBC/SurveyMonkey Women at Work Survey, while 20 percent of working women have nothing! This is a crusade, Pink Preppers. We have got to get our sisters to wake up and start saving for their future selves.

If you don't know where you stand, plug your numbers into one of the many retirement calculators available online. Try those at Nerdwallet. com, Bankrate.com and PersonalCapital.com.

The likelihood score is a minimum 3 for every woman unless you have a rock-solid source of income in retirement *and* a significant amount saved. Recall the normalcy bias? We are sure social security will always be there. At the rate the US government is printing money, I'm not so sure.

Have a pension? Forget what you were promised. According to the Pension Benefit Guaranty Corporation (a government agency) in its 2018 Projections Report, "About 125 of the 1,400 multi-employer plans that PBGC insures are in critical and declining status and have declared that they will be unable to raise contributions sufficiently to avoid insolvency over the next 20 years."

Pink Preppers, the person who cares the most about your retirement is you. Hope for the best, but plan for the worst. If you have little or nothing saved and no plan, increase the score to 4. If you are young, we can fix this. But every year that passes, it will get harder to catch up. Becoming a Pink Prepper will put you on the right path.

►Impact Score

You could argue that you'll get something from social security. And you could probably work at Walmart until you can no longer manage to drive yourself there. Or maybe you could become a burden to your children—there's a plan. Personally, I'm worried about being able to pay for a decent nursing home if I need it, so I see the impact of not having enough money as catastrophic. An eighty-year-old bag lady is not my future self if I can help it. This is a 5 for me. You do you, but chances are high you'll outlive your spouse. I can take old, solo, and vulnerable, but I'll be damned if I'll add broke.

HEALTH RISKS

If you aren't healthy, that trumps all. You don't have to be in the marathon runner category. You just need to be able to do what you want to without pain. And we need to work on getting you as healthy as possible for the next pandemic. COVID-19 hit the elderly and those with preexisting conditions the hardest. Who knows what the next one will do. If you have preexisting conditions we can mitigate now, then hell yeah, that is what we want to do.

According to the CDC, the top causes of death for women in the US in 2017 (the most recent figures I could find) are

- Heart disease: 21.8%
- Cancer (from all sources): 20.7%
- Chronic lower respiratory issues: 6.2%
- Stroke: 6.2%
- Alzheimer's disease: 6.1%

and it goes down from there.

Some of our health issues we can prevent; some we can influence; some we have little control over. But the healthier you are, the better you can cope with whatever life throws at you. Trust me—I know this.

I'm no competitive athlete. I'm athletic; I played sports in school, but nothing spectacular. I started jogging when I was in grad school so I could eat pizza and Little Debbie's and still fit into my jeans. I would jog about four miles a few times a week and that was it. I started lifting weights as well in my midtwenties. Life was good.

Then in my midthirties I started to have hip pain. I started walking instead of running. My hip kept hurting and I finally went to see a doctor. He almost immediately diagnosed it as arthritis (OA).

I sucked it up for ten more years. Walking five miles a day, five times a week, and lifting weights. Took Aleve when the pain was bad. Couldn't eat pizza and Little Debbie's as much but managed to still fit in my pants. But the pain was getting worse. I started to have problems sleeping at night. I took a trip to Chicago and halfway back to my hotel, it felt like my hip was going to give out. I decided I'd get physical therapy.

When the physical therapist saw my X-rays, he laughed and said we could do some exercises, but I needed a hip replacement. I was devastated. I was single, self-employed, and heard horror stories about the rehab. I lived in a three-story townhouse. How was I going to get up and down the stairs? How could I work? I'd never had any kind of surgery—I was only forty-five (young in arthritis years)—and I was freaking out.

During our first appointment, I asked my surgeon when I should get the hip replacement, and he said, "When the hip starts to make decisions for you." Well, it was already making decisions for me. And I wasn't going to be a slave to my hip for the rest of my life.

The surgery wasn't exactly fun (I was in the hospital for a few days), but the rehab was a breeze. I never even used crutches. When a physical therapist came to my home to help with the recovery, she was astonished and was asking for fitness tips. I'm nothing special, prepper. I was simply fit enough so when the unforeseen happened, I could get through it with relative ease.

That's what this book is all about. Did you know 31 percent of women up to age sixty-four, then 69 percent of women will get arthritis? Hopefully, yours won't impact you as much as mine did, but chances are, as you age you'll get arthritis.

If I had been obese (which 41% of American women are), rehab from a hip replacement would have been a far different story. Seriously overweight patients were struggling with even standing after surgery. The rehab was terrible for them. I had a second hip replacement three years later. I still walk five miles a day at least five times a week, and I still love Little Debbie's. (I also don't want to hear any crying from any of you about exercising—if I can get out there with two fake hips, you have no excuses.)

DISABILITY, HEALTH ISSUE

▶Likelihood Score

This is a purposely broad category. I'm defining a health issue as something you don't see coming, but that significantly impacts your life. It could be arthritis (31% up to 69% as we age), some form of cancer (38.7%), heart disease (47% of Americans have at least one of three risk factors—smoking, high blood pressure, high blood cholesterol—says the CDC). The number you assign here has a lot to do with your general health today, your age, and many other factors. Here is some guidance.

If you are under forty, a nonsmoker, in the normal weight range (the CDC has a healthy weight calculator and there are more at www.PinkPrep.

com), do not have high blood pressure or any other existing health issues, have a decent diet and get at least twenty minutes of exercise every day (150 minutes a week)—give yourself a 2—not very likely. If certain genetic issues run in your family or you have a super stressful life, you might want to assign a 3.

I'm giving myself a 3. I'm all the above, except I'm over forty and have arthritis.

If you are over forty, obese, don't meet the exercise requirement, and/or have high blood pressure or other preexisting conditions—then you're looking at a 4 or maybe even a 5. If your doctor has warned you, or you're already experiencing some serious symptoms, it's probably a 5.

The good news is some of these risk numbers can be lowered (part of Pink Prepping). This isn't about making you panic—it's about waking you up.

►Impact Score

My definition of health issue is something you don't see coming, but that significantly impacts your life. So, by the very nature of my definition, this is a minimum 3. Also consider your life as a whole. I work for myself; my income is dependent on my ability to go forth and speak. I need to be healthy to do that, so a health issue may have a bigger impact on my life than it might have on yours. However, you might have small children who are dependent on you or other important factors that influence your impact score. Someone who still lives with her parents might have a lower impact score than someone who supports herself. I'm giving this bad boy a 5.

PANDEMIC

►Likelihood Score

We lived through one and we will have another, according to the CDC: "While we can't predict exactly when or where the next epidemic or pandemic will begin, we know one is coming." We don't know if it will last as long or be as severe as COVID-19 or if it will be worse.

The CDC website said this:

> When a pathogen can travel from a remote village to major cities on all continents in 36 hours, the threat to our national security is greater than ever. Why are we at risk of local outbreaks turning into global pandemics?

- Increased risk of infectious pathogens "spilling over" from animals to humans
- Development of antimicrobial resistance
- Spread of infectious diseases through global travel and trade
- Acts of bioterrorism
- Weak public health infrastructures

Experts had been predicting something like COVID-19 since at least 2015. But did we listen? Nope, normalcy bias. Pink Preppers will not be caught off-guard again. Chances are, by the time we find out about the next one, it will already be here.

So, while it may not be this year, or the next, I'm giving this a 5.

▶ Impact Score

As I write this, I am still on lock-down during the COVID-19 pandemic. As far as I know, I have no preexisting conditions that increase my risk, but if I did, I might not survive this. I plan to do everything possible to continue to have no preexisting conditions for the next pandemic, but who knows? This has impacted every aspect of my life and work, and it could kill me. I'm giving this one a 5.

TRAVEL RISKS

I'm defining travel as anytime you are away from home, even if you just ran down to Target to grab some Doritos. So unless you never leave your house, read this section.

CAR CRASH

▶ Likelihood Score

This is a tricky one to assess. If you drive a lot, you are more likely to be in an accident than someone who drives less. If you are an aggressive driver, you are more likely to be in an accident. If you drink and drive or text and drive, you are more likely to be in an accident. If you are a young (less experienced) driver, you are more likely to be in an accident. According to Esurance, 77 percent of drivers have been in at least one accident. The average driver has three to four accidents over their lifetime.

If you are sixteen or seventeen or in your first year of driving, I'm going to say this is a 3 for any given year. For the rest of us, I'm going to say this is a 1. If Uber or Lyft is your thing—I'm keeping it at 1 (although some of those drivers are maniacs).

▶ Impact Score

Women are less likely than men to have car accidents, but more likely to die in them. Impact is a 5.

CAR TROUBLE

▶Likelihood Score

Another tough one to assess. I'd say it depends on your car, but in my story I told earlier, I had car trouble with a brand-new car. (My guess is when I had the oil changed, they forgot to put new oil in.) Over the years, I've had three flat tires, a dead battery, the random oil incident, and even had to abandon my car once when it was too icy to drive it. I've known people who have run out of gas (clearly not Pink Preppers). I'm going to give this one a 3—may or may not happen. If you drive a beater, however, you might need to increase this to 4.

▶Impact Score

Most car trouble is a 2 (minor impact) if you drive a decent car and change the oil regularly. A repair shouldn't occur often at all, and if it does, it should not be major. If you drive an older car and don't take care of it, you need to assign a higher score. You might have more costly repairs and have to find alternate transportation from time to time.

CRIME

▶Likelihood Score

The chance of your home being broken into varies based on where you live, but, overall, it's quite low—less than 1 percent. However, according to a Global Business Travel Association and AIG Travel survey released in the fall of 2019, 83 percent of women reported concerns about their safety while on a business trip in the previous year. This is why I address crime here. I'll give you home protection ideas later, but, generally, home break-ins are unlikely to happen to most people.

During my travels, people have tried to steal my wallet; someone tried to get into my hotel room; creepy panhandlers have approached me and so on. When you are traveling, you are often in unfamiliar surroundings. You might be alone. You are simply more vulnerable than usual. And if 83 percent of us admit to being worried, I'm giving it a 2. It's not likely (unless you are traveling someplace dangerous), but we need to be better prepared while away from home. Unless you never leave your dwelling, this is a 2. If you travel a lot, you might want to score it higher—I'm giving it a 3.5.

▶ **Impact Score**

Because this could be anything from theft to assault or murder, I'm giving it a 5.

FLIGHT DELAYS

▶ **Likelihood Score**

Been there, and 20 percent of all flights are delayed by fifteen minutes or more. But this means that 80 percent of all flights are on time or have short delays. So this is only a 2—not very likely.

▶ **Impact Score**

For me, flight delays can be a 3, but this is because of the nature of my work. For most of you, the impact will be less. If you never fly—zero.

LITTLE AND BIG DISASTERS

When I hear disaster, I think of something big—like hurricanes or massive wildfires. The Red Cross defines disaster as—

A sudden, calamitous event that seriously disrupts the functioning of a community or society and causes human, material, and economic or environmental losses that exceed the community's or society's ability to cope using its own resources. Though often caused by nature, disasters can have human origins.

Oxford dictionary defines disaster as "a sudden event, such as an accident or a natural catastrophe, that causes great damage or loss of life."

Since this book is for individuals, a house fire qualifies as a disaster. It's sudden and could cause extensive damage and injury or loss of life. The chances of a house fire are low, but the prep to help avoid one is easy.

When reviewing the National Safety Council's statistics, I was surprised to find greater household dangers are poisoning (so high because deaths due to opioid overdose are included) and falls. (Even drowning and choking kill more people than fires.) Deaths due to falls are especially high for those sixty-five and older. You might be a spring chicken, but your mom or grandma might not be. And you can do the Pink Prep for them.

You may believe you won't fall, but I've fallen three times in the past year. Once I was fooling around in the driveway with my dogs and there was a small patch of ice. I didn't think anything of it until I slipped and landed hard. I only hurt my ego, but I'm telling you, the older you get, the more a fall can seriously hurt you.

The second time I fell, I was out walking a trail I walk every day. I wasn't paying attention, slipped on some loose stones, and went down so hard and so fast, my chin slammed into the ground. I had rocks embedded in my hands. It was an ugly fall. The third time I fell, I was carrying a heavy box downstairs. It was a big box, and I couldn't see the stairs below me. I missed the last one. Ouch. So if you're fifty-plus, falls need to be a concern.

One final story so you realize how important this is. I used to live in an apartment. One night, I came home late and heard someone calling for help. It was faint, but it was definitely a cry for help. I watch a lot of true crime, so I knew better than to run over myself (the attacker might still be there). First, I called the complex maintenance guy—no answer. Then I saw another woman arrive and approached her. I asked if she could hear the cries (which she could) and if she would go with me to check it out.

We followed the cries and found a dear old lady crumpled in the doorway of her apartment. She said she had been there for hours. We stayed with her, and I held her hand as we waited for the ambulance. The thing I remember most was a picture of her and her husband, young and smiling on their wedding day. It was black and white, and he was in a military uniform. It was so sad that no one had come to help her sooner, that she was in such pain (she had broken her hip in the fall), and that she was alone. She recovered and her family moved her out, but I'll never forget her. Falls are a greater risk for most of us than criminals or fires.

Need some stats from the CDC to back this up?

- More than one out of four older people fall each year. (I fell three times.) Less than half tell their doctor. I haven't told mine.
- One out of five falls causes a serious injury such as broken bones or a head injury. And fractures can lead to permanent disability and death.

- Over 800,000 people a year are hospitalized because of a fall injury, most because of a head injury or a hip fracture.
- Falls are the most common cause of traumatic brain injuries. Not car or motorcycle accidents—falls.
- An older American dies every nineteen minutes from a fall.
- Falling once doubles your chances of falling again. Great.

Do not underestimate what a fall can do to you.

▶ Likelihood Score

If you have fallen before, this is a 3. If you haven't fallen and are under sixty-five, I'd say 1. If you haven't fallen before and are over sixty-five, score is 2. Consider your mom and grandma here too—spread the word. Falls are a big deal.

▶ Impact Score

I give this a 5—even if you're young, a fall can seriously hurt you.

HOUSE FIRE

▶ Likelihood Score

Back to house fires. There is a less than 1 percent chance you will have a house fire, but if you listen to the sellers of fire alarms, it sounds much worse. They'll say, "There are 1.3 million house fires in the US each year." They don't say there are over 138 million homes in the US. Obviously if your house is the one that had the fire, this is devastating, but the chances of it happening to any one of us are small. So it gets a 1—probably not.

▶ Impact Score

Impact of this is 5—people could die.

POWER OUTAGE

▶Likelihood Score

This is dependent on where you live. I live in a rural area and have regular power surges and brief outages. In most places, outages have to do with the weather. Here in North Carolina, during a bad winter storm or hurricane, we may lose power. We lost power for two days one winter and that was all it took to motivate us to buy a generator.

But power loss is not only related to weather. The National Infrastructure Advisory Council's 2018 report reads:

> The NIAC was tasked to examine the nation's ability to withstand a catastrophic power outage. Unlike severe weather disasters, a catastrophic power outage may occur with little or no notice and result from myriad scenarios . . . The type of event contemplated will include not only an extended loss of power, but also a cascading loss of other critical services—drinking water and wastewater systems, communications, financial services, transportation, fuel, healthcare, and others—which may slow recovery and impede re-energizing the grid. The NIAC found that our existing plans, response resources, and coordination strategies would be outmatched by an event of this severity. Significant action is needed to prepare for a catastrophic power outage that could last for weeks or months.

Can you say, "Holy Pink Prep, girlfriend?" This reads like experts crying pandemic in 2015 and no one listening. Here are experts warning us that our power grid is vulnerable. Does this surprise anyone given how we have neglected our bridges and roads in some areas? No one wants to fund infrastructure—it's so boring.

You may not feel anything this extreme will happen, but a power outage is something we all should prepare for, so I'm giving it a 5. (In 2021, Texas had a grid crash after an unexpected winter storm. There will be similar events, Pink Prepper.)

►Impact Score

The impact of this depends on the length of time the power is out and your situation. If it's out for two days, you will lose the perishable food in your refrigerator and freezer. If you have the money to replace everything and can stay warm/cool, this might be a 2. If you have small children who are freezing and hungry or an elderly person on oxygen, this might be a 3 or 4.

If the entire power grid goes down, that's a completely different matter. We'd see far more societal disruption than occurred during the COVID-19 pandemic. There would be widespread food and water shortages, emergency services would be overwhelmed, and there would be lawlessness. (There was mass looting after Katrina.) This would be a 4.5 to 5.

Because this makes me nervous, I'm going with 4. I'd suggest 2.5 as a minimum.

NATURAL DISASTER

►Likelihood Score

This one is also dependent upon where you live. In North Carolina, we get hurricanes, but I live inland. Tornadoes will be a part of your life if you live in Oklahoma. You might worry about earthquakes if you live in California. Droughts can be a problem in the western US. Floods can be an issue in many places. Please tell me you know if your house is in a flood zone or not: https://msc.fema.gov/portal/home. You may also live near a dam. Do a web search for National Inventory of Dams and go to the Army Corps of Engineers site. (Sign in as General Public and use the Interactive Map & Charts to check out your county.)

My little ol' county here in North Carolina has sixty dams. The average age is sixty-six years. Who knew? Two are in my neighborhood! Pink Preppers must know what's out there so they can prepare.

You can also check out the US Natural Hazards Index on the National Center for Disaster Preparedness website to see what events are likely in your county: https://ncdp.columbia.edu/library/mapsmapping-projects/us-natural-hazards-index/

In general, this is a 1. If you want to increase that number based on where you live, please do so.

►Impact Score
This is a 5. With my luck, it will be my house that gets crushed in the tornado/landslide/asteroid hit.

HAZARDOUS MATERIALS/NUCLEAR INCIDENT

►Likelihood Score
You may live near a highway where a truck hauling hazardous materials could flip over and rock your world. Maybe you live close to a fertilizer plant that could explode. Or the Union Pacific mainline hauling hazardous material by train that can be derailed. Or you bought a new home on Love Canal. Now that you're thinking like a Pink Prepper, check out a couple of websites to see if there's anything to worry about and then move on:

http://www.toxicsites.us/

www.fmcsa.dot.gov When you get to the site, open the pull-down menu under Safety. Click on Hazardous Materials. This page has a menu with a link to the National HM (Hazardous Materials) Route Registry.

When I started learning what was around me, I discovered I live near a nuclear plant. Wake up, Pink Prepper.

►**Impact Score**

I have one word for you—Chernobyl. The impact of these events could be catastrophic. This is a 5.

WAR/TERRORISM/ACTIVE SHOOTER

►**Likelihood Score**

While you often hear about active shooter situations, the likelihood of being in one is exceedingly small. The same is true for terrorism in the US. That said, I went to the Atlanta Olympics the day after the bombing and to Oklahoma City days after that bombing. Some of you may have been in Boston during the marathon bombing or in New York or DC on 9/11.

I'm not downplaying the impact of these events. And it's possible being in NY or DC increases the likelihood that you would be in such an event again. Terrorists aren't going to attack twelve people in Paducah. If the world changes and we go to war, the likelihood could increase. Currently, you have higher priorities. This has a likelihood score of 1.

►**Impact Score**

No doubt this is a 5.

OTHER RISKS

Traditional preppers also plan for these risks:

- Widespread civil unrest
- Economic collapse
- Widespread food shortage
- Nuclear disaster
- Abrupt climate change
- Super volcano
- Asteroid/meteor strike
- Zombie apocalypse

These are far more unlikely than the events we've covered. However, if you would like to include any of these in your prepping—go for it. There are resources listed at the end of the book to help.

8

STEPS THREE AND FOUR IN PINK PREP—PRIORITIZE THE RISKS AND INCREASE YOUR KNOWLEDGE

After you've plugged your likelihood and impact scores into the grid, multiply the numbers together and get your risk score. (Multiply the number in column C by the number in column D and write that number in column E.) I found this exercise fascinating. Some risks are so unlikely to happen I can quit worrying about them. Others I need to do a better job of addressing (um, falls). Feel free to adjust your scores if you like. This is your guide. Never forget the normalcy bias—our arch enemy.

The largest numbers get the highest ranking in column F. If you have scores that are tied, list them in your priority order. For example, I had a three-way tie between not enough for retirement, car crash, and flight delay. I'm most worried about the first one, so I'm ranking it higher, followed by flight delay, then car crash. Rank your list, and you adjust it as you read further or as your life changes. Review it annually.

Pick your top three risks. These are the ones to start with. I'm going to give you tips for all the risks, but I want you to stay focused. For example, if your top risks are financial, don't get distracted by a power outage and invest in a generator. Start with your greatest risks and work your way down. If you read a tip that you'd like to implement, make sure it doesn't increase a higher priority risk. (Don't use up your retirement savings, for example, by buying a zombie-stopping crossbow.)

Congratulations! You've completed the first three steps in Pink Prep. You've (1) gotten your head in the game, (2) assessed your risks, and (3) prioritized those risks based on your unique situation. Now it's time to move to step four and increase your knowledge.

In the upcoming chapters, I provide tips to help you prepare for each of the risks. You can read through all (you might pick up an idea or two) or go directly to your highest priority risks and read those sections. As always, you do you. Implement the ideas that fit with your lifestyle, values, and budget. My goal is to get you ready for the bad things you don't see coming.

Pink Prep Principle: Preparation = Confidence.

9

RELATIONSHIP PREP

Wise ol' Benjamin Franklin said, "An ounce of prevention is worth a pound of cure," and I completely agree. So, yes, you should do what you can to make your relationship work. But this is not a book about relationships; it's a book about being ready for the worst. And sometimes, despite all your best efforts, your relationship ends. My goal is to ensure you are prepared if this happens.

If you are ready for the worst, it makes you a better partner. If you depend on your spouse for everything, it can make you clingy and desperate (not attractive or desirable traits). Independence is sexy. No one person can fulfill all your needs anyway. Expecting that puts too much pressure on a relationship. If someone has to carry you, they may one day decide the burden is too much. Have the power to walk on your own.

Even if you believe everything in your relationship is perfect, I know many women who felt the same (normalcy bias) and got blindsided. They were stunningly unprepared for the havoc the ending of their relationships would wreak on their lives. That will not be you, Pink Prepper.

Divorce

Almost half of all marriages end in divorce. And everyone thinks it's not going to happen to her. Tonya was divorced when she met a wealthy, successful man who swept her off her feet. A big diamond and swanky house later, she's ready for babies. She was getting to the age where it was use it or lose it, so having babies was high on her priority list. (Your marriage will change significantly after you have children, prepper, and not always in positive ways. And if you ever consider getting pregnant to trap or keep a man, slap yourself. Twice.)

Anyway, children soon arrive, and the marriage is strained. It starts to crumble when her husband's business takes a significant downturn. Did I mention she was a full-time mom, unwilling to go back to work? As the lifestyle fell apart, so did the marriage. Now past midlife, Tonya has gutted her retirement funds and maxed out her credit cards trying to maintain her predivorce lifestyle.

Kecia had no idea about her family finances. Childhood sweethearts, she and her hubby had wonderful children, multiple homes, and a wonderful life. In her late forties with two children in college, she learned her husband was in business trouble and they were in danger of losing everything. They had to sell most of their assets and a divorce soon followed. She was left to start over with nothing.

My friend Julie had a thriving business and was the main breadwinner for her family. She and her husband attended a church that advised the woman should respect the man and somehow this equated to giving him complete control over all the family money. (I kid you not, the church basically preached if the woman loved the man, she would respect him enough to do this.) I begged her not to do it, to at least keep some of *her* money in a separate account. But who am I to argue with someone's church? Not only did he spend all *their* money, he also opened a credit card in her name and bankrupted them both. She divorced with a small son to raise, a mountain of debt, and ruined credit.

All three started out head over heels in love. All three smart women were absolutely clueless about the family finances. They will never make up the ground they lost in preparing for their own retirements.

Mary went through a horrific divorce. She and her husband were childhood sweethearts. She worked to put him through college. Together they built what seemed like a perfect life. She stayed home with the children; they lived at the country club—whee! They played golf, had parties. He cheated and she was devastated. He had the money and the power, hired an attorney skilled at hiding assets, and that was it.

Mary had to work at a grocery store ringing up the purchases of her former golfing partners. She moved into a small house and held it together for her kids. She put herself through college and worked incredibly hard. Her ex got remarried on her birthday. The whole thing almost broke her. I want you to remember the lesson here. Do get married, do give your whole heart, do everything you can to make it work—but also be prepared in case it doesn't.

If I still can't convince you, you may be thinking, "Well, all of those women are not me. My marriage will never fail." Even if it doesn't, you will probably outlive your husband. Being prepared means you can take care of yourself and your dependents when the unexpected happens. Doing the recommended divorce prep will also help you if a bus hits your beloved or he keels over with a heart attack at work.

If you aren't married yet, prep for divorce going in. I know, I know. You're thinking, "Oh my gosh, that is so not romantic. What a Debbie Downer." Nope, I'm a grown-up and it's time for you to join the club. Getting married is a big freaking deal, and you need to treat it like such.

My stepson Brett is home after being stationed in Italy. He had a super romantic wedding to a gorgeous Italian girl. Their marriage lasted about seventeen months, and she's trying to get maintenance payments for the rest of her life. They are twenty-two. It's been a huge legal nightmare. People can mess you up when you enter legal agreements with them. Take your life seriously.

Grown-ups should have tough discussions about how you want to handle your finances. Discussions about the other person's credit (or lack thereof). If your partner won't get financially naked with you and show you everything, run away. Or at least don't marry them. If they say, "Just trust me," don't. If they love you, they should have no problem showing you their credit report and you should show them yours.

Make sure you both agree on how you're going to handle the money. I know couples who keep their money separate and have a joint account for common expenses. If you have no source of income and plan to not work (maybe you are going to stay home with kids), you need to ask your spouse how you are going to access their money. Find out how they might feel if you pulled out $5,000 and didn't ask permission. What are their expectations of your spending? I promise you they have them. That whole "my money is your money" works until you start spending what they feel is too much of their money.

Pink Prep recommendation: Nolo.com is an invaluable source of legal information. Hiring an attorney is best, but educating yourself first is crucial. Check out the Nolo website, read articles, download books. You'll find information on everything from marriage and divorce to buying a home to estate planning. Pink Preppers are nobody's fools—they do their homework and don't get taken.

Realize that staying home with the children (as Tonya did) impacts you in two ways: (1) you have no money of your own, and (2) your money-earning skills atrophy. Unless you are working from home, you are losing skills and valuable connections. You also aren't putting any money away for your retirement or anything else.

Before you choose this path, talk with your beloved and see how this can work for both of you. Do you have unfettered and unquestioned access to their money? Is your name on all accounts? Do you have joint ownership of your home? Will you come up with a budget together and as long as you spend within those guidelines is that okay?

You need at a minimum to be able to check account balances and get money when you need it. And the best time to discuss all this is before you get married.

If you are already married, you need to know everything about your household finances. How much money do you both have and where is it? If you don't understand investing and simply let your husband handle everything, get a grip. You have a brain and you need to use it. What if something happens to him? What if he starts playing online poker or fantasy football and loses a bunch of money?

This is way too important to not understand. If he loves you, he'll be delighted to show you everything. If he loves you, he'll want you to be able to take care of things if a tree limb falls on him while he's riding his bike in the park or something goes horribly wrong during his next attempt at household repair.

Best Pink Prepper move—you be in charge. I hold an MBA and I have a good head for numbers (you probably do, too, but you may just have some inaccurate beliefs getting in your way). I'm also highly organized and am like a dog with a bone when it comes to my money. I work hard for it, and I want to get the most value for it. I review all my statements and reconcile them with the receipts. I rebalance my investment portfolio. I never pay fees or late charges. I am 100 percent debt-free.

Guys have always been fine with me keeping up with the money—takes the burden off them. Pinkie, this is where you want to be. Large and in charge and aware of everything that is going on. I pay all our household bills and tell my beloved how much he owes me every month. All our money is separate, except we have joint ownership of our home.

Remember Jessie? This is where I have her too—she basically tells Joey (her husband) how much he needs to contribute to savings each month. She pays all the bills out of their joint account, and he even asks her before he makes any purchases outside their budget. If I could have all of you in that position, I'd be thrilled.

Have some of your own money. I know, you are in love, his money is your money. Well, when Brett told us he was getting a divorce, the first thing I told him to do was lock down his bank account. Two days later, his soon-to-be ex-wife threw a fit when she couldn't get money. That's how it happens. The main account holder can get your access card cut off with a phone call.

What should she have done? She should have had her own account. At one point in the marriage, she was giving Italian lessons and earned a few hundred dollars. She should have kept it separate. But it was a solid idea: get a side gig and all the money is yours to keep. Other ideas: ask your beloved to let you keep whatever money you save from the budget you both create. Ask for a small monthly amount of play money and bank it. Find a way to have some of your own money. I am not saying have secrets. I'm saying be prepared.

Now, before you consider me the devil, selling out a member of the sisterhood, Brett was the sole earner. If his wife had contributed, I would have advised him to lock it down and send her her share. I'm telling you this because seventeen months before, she was in love and riding off into the sunset. Now her ATM card won't work. Don't let this happen to you.

Keep learning. If you do stop working, whatever your field is, stay engaged. The world changes so rapidly. If you disengage for several years, you will be obsolete by the time you reenter the workforce.

Devote a couple of hours a week to networking with former colleagues or watching a webinar—anything you can do to stay sharp. This will keep you valuable *and* keep you interesting to your beloved. This is wise advice even if you are working. Keep increasing your knowledge and value—you can never go wrong investing in yourself.

Maintain and build your network. Don't get isolated. You'll need your friends if something happens. But if you have limited time, be strategic. Don't just hang out with the mommies because it's easy. Make time for your best colleague who can keep you in the loop. Have at least one friend who will tell you what you *need* to hear, not only what you *want* to hear. She is worth her weight in gold.

Have a hobby or interest that is yours alone and that brings you joy. It can be easy to lose yourself in a relationship. Make sure you keep some of you. If the only hobbies you have are also his hobbies, doing them after a split won't be the same. Keep growing as a person in your own right. You will not regret it.

Death of Partner

I know, I know—how morbid. But if you are building a life with someone, you have to deal with this possibility. It's a pain to do all this, but it will be a bigger pain if you don't. Do you want to face the decision to pull the plug without discussing your partner's wishes first? I don't know about you, but I sure as hell don't want to be a vegetable. I'd rather decide now and not put my loved ones in that horrible position.

If you don't have a complicated estate, you can do all this inexpensively by using the tools at Nolo.com. I used their software to draft my own will as well as all the other documents I discuss in this chapter. Print them, get them notarized, and you are good to go.

If you don't feel comfortable doing it yourself, don't want to, or your estate is complex, hire a lawyer to prepare everything. It's important and you need to do it. If you have children, you need to do this for them.

You need to do everything as you would to prep for divorce, plus make certain both of you have the following documents in order and where the key people can find them:

Last will and testament: There may be sentimental items your partner wishes specific people to have. Get that in writing now. Here's the scary thing: after someone dies, people come out of the woodwork wanting items or money. If you are a second wife, get this all documented and consider informing children from the first marriage (when they are old enough) what decisions have been made while your spouse is still alive. It would be terrible if your stepchildren expected to get the family home, and it was left to you and is your primary residence. Discuss, understand, and document your and your beloved's wishes. Then inform those who should know. It will help everyone prep.

Durable power of attorney: This allows your spouse (or your life partner—Tim and I each have one naming the other) to handle your legal affairs if you can no longer make decisions. Let's say my beloved is in a motorcycle accident and I need to call the insurance company. If I don't have this, they may not talk to me. These are important preps to make, or if the time comes, you won't be able to do what needs to be done.

Healthcare power of attorney and living will: This document gives you (or your beloved) the power to make healthcare decisions if one of you can no longer do so for yourself. You can make this as specific as you want. For example, I don't want anyone to pull the plug if I've been out of it for an hour, but after forty-eight hours, if the docs say there's zero chance—set me free. You can say never, ever pull the plug. You do you.

But if you don't put this in writing, you leave a terrible decision to those you love. Or, in my case, since we aren't married, if Tim didn't have this document, he might not be able to make a decision for me. Being a Pink Prepper means making hard decisions—for yourself.

Revocable living trust: If you have significant assets, you should consider a trust. It can protect your heirs from the legal expense and delay of probate. It can also help with taxes. Learn about it but call a pro for assistance.

Letter of intent: Do you want them to play "Bad to the Bone" at your funeral? Want to be cremated? This is how you let people know. I'm a fan of cremation (the whole coffin thing creeps me out). I was talking about this with Tim and was surprised to learn he wanted to be buried next to his mom. I said, "Seriously? Then we need to get that plot." Sometimes men prep for the most exciting (zombie attack) instead of the most practical (their eventual demise).

Let's face it; there is a 100 percent chance he will die. Decide what you want, put it in a letter of intent. No one can read your mind (especially after you're dead).

Life insurance: Personally, I don't have any life insurance. I'll be leaving more than enough money to cover my funeral. I have no kids. Why do I need life insurance? However, if your spouse is your primary means of support and/or you have kids, your beloved needs to have some life insurance. If you are the main breadwinner and need to provide for your partner and your children, you need life insurance.

Beneficiaries: Make sure you are listed as the beneficiary on any retirement, bank, and investment accounts. It's easy to forget about this and it can cause big problems later. Those listings will override the will. Ex-wife still listed as a beneficiary? Ex-wife is getting the money. Bam. Do the prep.

Contacts/social media: Do you have access to all the contacts you'll need? This includes the people you'll need to notify about his or her passing, business and financial contacts, legal and medical. Do you have passwords to online accounts? Do you even know about all the online accounts? How do you want to handle their social media accounts?
We all need a digital estate plan—to tell whoever is dealing with our passing what we want done with our social media accounts and any websites or blogs we have. It's creepy when Facebook tells you it's a person's birthday whom you know is deceased. I'd rather not haunt people in this way. Ugh.

At Everplans.com there is a list of actions like these for those who are left behind:

- Archiving personal files, photos, videos, and other content they created
- Deleting files from their computer or other devices, or erasing devices' hard drives
- Maintaining certain online accounts, which may include paying for services to continue (such as web hosting services)
- Closing certain online accounts, such as social media accounts, subscription services, or any accounts that are paid for (such as Amazon Prime)
- Transferring any transferrable accounts to heirs
- Collecting and transferring any money or usable credits to heirs
- Transferring any income-generating items (websites, blogs, affiliate accounts) to heirs
- Informing any online communities or online friends of their death

My Netflix account could go on charging my credit card for years. Details, details, details.

List of important documents: Nolo's book, *Get It Together, Organize Your Records So Your Family Won't Have To,* contains a comprehensive list of everything you'll need when your beloved passes (or your beloved will need when you pass). It covers everything from bank records to birth certificates.

Keep all your important documents someplace safe. Put the originals in a fireproof safe in case something happens (break-in, fire) when you're not home. You could also keep them in a safe deposit box, but if SHTF, you might not be able to get to them. In the safe, keep them in a fireproof/waterproof envelope you can grab if you have to bug out. As an extra layer of protection, scan them and store them on a zip drive you keep in your Get Home Bag or vehicle bag.

Think this is nuts? Let's say you are out of town. You get a terrible phone call that there's been a fire. Your home is destroyed and your husband is in the hospital. You rush back and go straight there. His family surrounds him. The prognosis is bad, he was terribly burned. After two days on life support, the doctors tell you he will never recover. You know his wishes; he would not want to be in a vegetative state for years to come. After several months, you feel it's best to set him free. But your healthcare power of attorney was destroyed in the fire. His family could launch a long legal battle to keep him "alive."

If you had your zip drive with the healthcare power of attorney, you could tell these people to stand down. Taking care of all this now will give you power when you need it most.

If you outlive your spouse, you'll be dealing with your and your children's grief as well as taking care of all the details. The more you can do before it happens, the better off you will be. Remember, Pink Prepper, you are likely to outlive your spouse. Pull all this together, then forget about it until you have a major life change. Doing it is an inconvenience, but not doing it could be devastating.

Abuse

In his excellent book, *The Gift of Fear: Survival Signals that Protect Us from Violence*, Gavin de Becker says violence is predictable. He has a list of indicators of spousal abuse and murder. Not all of them are present every time, but if you see more than one, prepper, dump that man! These are indicators of violence—don't excuse them away, ignore them, or hope that your love will change him, unless you want to be featured in an upcoming episode of *Dateline*—then go right ahead.

I'm going to use male pronouns here because most violence is perpetrated by males. But if you are with a woman who exhibits any of these traits, dump her too.

Here they are:

- Your gut tells you he is dangerous or something just doesn't seem right.
- He rushed things—talking about love, marriage, living together way too soon.
- He can't talk things out. If you have a disagreement, he turns nasty or violent.
- He says things that make you feel terrible.
- He uses threats to control you.
- He throws or breaks objects.
- He's been violent in past relationships.
- His behavior is negatively altered by drinking or taking drugs. Having a couple of beers doesn't count. Getting drunk and calling you names does.
- He blames the substances for his bad behavior. (It was Johnnie Walker who kicked you, not me.)
- He has had run-ins with the police for bad behavior toward others. (The best indicator of future behavior is past behavior.)
- He uses money to control you.
- He is jealous of anyone who gets any of your time. He might want you to let him know where you are at all times. He will try to isolate you.
- He won't take no for an answer.
- He says things like "we'll be together forever" and "nothing will keep us apart."

- He makes light of the abuse.
- He will try to get your friends or family to help him keep your relationship.
- He may have watched or stalked you. He may have gone through your phone or possessions.
- He thinks people are out to get him.
- Compromise—ha! He is inflexible. It's his way or the highway.
- He thinks violence is justified and may compare himself to people on TV who use violence.
- He may have mood swings and be withdrawn, joyless, or furious.
- He blames everyone for his problems but himself. He takes no ownership of his actions.
- He may collect weapons or talk about them all the time.
- He thinks women exist to serve men. Or at least you exist to serve him.
- He was abused or witnessed abuse as a child.

If you are with a man and some of these ring true, I beg you to get out. If you are dating someone and rationalizing these, please understand they will escalate. And don't you deserve better? If you're okay, but you worry about a friend, give her the list when he can't see it/find it. And if you have daughters, go over this with them. Young women's feelings of insecurity have skyrocketed as use of social media has increased. If a young woman feels insecure and is desperate for approval, she is the perfect target for these losers.

Gavin de Becker says the first time a woman is hit, she is a victim, and the second time, she is a volunteer. He calls spousal murders "America's most predictable murders." He understands this topic quite well—he watched his mother be beaten by his father and works with abused women to get them out of abusive relationships. I believe if you stay with someone who treats you badly long enough, you start to feel it's normal or you deserve it.

For more information, read the *Washington Post* story, "Domestic Slayings: Brutal and Foreseeable." You'll see photos of children being raised by their grandparents because their father killed their mother. You'll learn about the many women who decided to not press charges because they were dependent on their abuser (he was their babysitter or their source of income or he stole their self-confidence). Or they "loved" him. Most domestic violence victims are not cooperative with law enforcement.

Pink Prepper, I beg you to run at the warning signs. Your love is not going to change anyone. One of the strongest indicators that an abusive relationship will turn fatal is attempted strangulation. (Law enforcement and other welfare agencies are now trained to look for its signs.)

If that ever happens to you, your life is in extreme danger. The article says women often underestimate their risk of being killed. If you won't leave for yourself, leave for your children or your parents or for all the good you will do in the world. The best advice is to do everything possible to avoid these jerks in the first place. Leave at the first red flag. Once you get emotionally involved, it's harder.

I was on a first Match.com date with a doctor. He was handsome and seemed like a catch until he mentioned his ex-wife had taken a restraining order out on him. He said it was all a big misunderstanding. My face changed instantly, and he said, "You're not going to go out with me again, are you?"

And I said, "No, I'm not."

Awkward rest of the date, for sure, but that was all I needed to know. If a guy treated his ex-wife badly, why would you want to be next? Why even take a chance? There are millions of men out there who haven't had restraining orders taken out against them. The sooner you end the relationship, the easier it is. Run, Pink Prepper, run!

While the best thing is to avoid an abuser, if you implement the recommendations for divorce prep, you would be in a position (have money and a network) to leave a relationship that became abusive. A goal of Pink Prep is to be able to survive without the one you love.

The National Domestic Violence Hotline is 1-800-799-SAFE (7233). They are experts at dealing with this and can give you a place to start if you are experiencing abuse. They can also help if you suspect someone else is being abused. Please believe me—no man is worth your unhappiness, much less your life.

Betrayal

How you handle betrayal is up to you. It is my job to help you be prepared, should it happen. Being prepared means you can choose your response. If you are not prepared (meaning you are completely dependent on your partner), you can't leave (or kick him out) and therefore do not have a choice. If you have your own money and a network of friends, you have options and can choose. The advice here is the same as for abuse and divorce—have some money and maintain connections.

Caz quit her job and moved across the country to be with Mr. Right after a whirlwind long-distance romance. She moved into his fabulous apartment and all her friends were completely jealous. He was handsome and fun and told her she didn't have to work. Selfies of the gorgeous, happy couple were posted.

At first Caz would straighten the house, explore the area, and be home in time to make dinner. Mr. Right would ask where she had gone that day, but she thought he was just showing how much he cared. She soon got bored and decided to look for work. When she told Mr. Right, he told her he didn't want her to work. Their discussion escalated into their first major fight. She decided she was lucky he would support her financially and let it go.

Mr. Right had a high-paying job and after their first six months together, he started spending extra hours at the office. At home he was often texting and distracted. His explanation was that things were busy at work. Caz felt they were drifting apart and wanted to do something to surprise him, to bring the fun back. She decided to take a picnic lunch to his office. As she approached the building, she saw him come out and greet a woman. They embraced and kissed deeply. Caz was devastated. The late nights and texts made more sense now. As the couple walked off hand in hand, the full impact of her situation hit Caz. She had no friends here, no job, and she lived with a cheater.

Luckily, Caz had kept one of her bank accounts and had some extra money. There had been red flags (he didn't want her to work, he rushed the relationship, he kept tabs on her). When she discovered the cheating, Caz was strong enough to leave. She maintained contact with her old friends who welcomed her back with open arms.

If someone betrays you, you may decide to stay and work it out. Keep in mind the best indicator of future behavior is past behavior. Only stay if you are sure you won't lose yourself. Suspicion and jealousy can eat away at the strongest of us. There is no greater power than the ability to walk away—and that's a power I want all my Pink Preppers to have.

Other Family Crisis

A family crisis is tough to plan for because they could be anything. Your child could get in legal trouble. One of your parents could get Alzheimer's. Your cousin Bob could lose his home. How could you possibly prepare for such?

- **Take care of your own health.** These episodes are stressful, and if you are healthy, you will be in a better position to cope.
- **Take care of your finances.** If you have extra money, you can offer help if desired. If you are already broke, you can't help in a crisis.
- **Develop protective boundaries.** If you want to help your third cousin twice removed make her house payment, you go right ahead. But recognize that money will not be going toward your retirement. You teach people how to treat you, Pink Preppers. If you loan money to someone and they don't pay it back, the next time they want money, the answer should be no. The first time you were a victim, the second, a volunteer.
- **Become skilled at saying no.** Men are often better at this than women. When you ask your husband if he wants to go with you to see your mom, he might say, "No, I've got work." And moves on. If he asks if you want to see his family, you might be thinking, "Will he be upset if I say no? I've got work, too, and we always see his family. But his mother already thinks I don't visit enough. What will she think if I don't go? Should I go? I actually do need to work, but—" And on and on and on.
- Sometimes I say yes and sometimes I say no, but I consider all the ramifications much more than he does. And women are judged more harshly when we say no. But it is worth it. You only live once, and we should spend as much of our lives as we can doing what we want. And that means saying no to what we don't want.
- **Don't enable.** I look first at how much someone has tried to help themselves before I step in. Why should I give my time

and money to help someone who hasn't tried at all to help themselves? That is enabling. It also makes you a pushover. Why would someone work hard if they can come to you for whatever they need?

Putting yourself last in your own life is a terrible plan. If you do this often enough, everyone else will put you last too. Unless you have infinite resources, help those who first try to help themselves and *never* give what you can't afford—not money, time, or emotion.

FINANCIAL PREP

COVID-19 shut down my business. Indoor gatherings were canceled, so being a professional speaker was off the table. I moved to virtual programs, but my revenues took a big and completely unexpected hit. It was like being fired. I went from hero to zero almost overnight.

I'm projecting a loss of almost two years of income. And I'm not the only one—currently over 15 percent of Americans are unemployed (*Fortune* says the real unemployment rate is closer to 24 percent). Some 88 percent of Americans said the COVID-19 pandemic put stress on their personal finance (*Kiplinger's Personal Finance*), and 41 percent said the stress was due to inadequate savings; 39 percent said job insecurity; and 28 percent cited problems paying the rent or mortgage. This unexpected financial hardship came out of nowhere.

Could you handle losing your job overnight? If you aren't the primary breadwinner, could you handle the overnight loss of your partner's job?

For most people, the answer is no. For me, the answer is yes (or I wouldn't be writing this book, I'd be trying to get a job delivering for Amazon). I want the answer to become yes for you as well. Because, dear Pink Prepper, having extra money is the best prep you can make for just about anything—divorce, health issues, job loss, family crisis, natural disaster—you name it.

Hopefully at this point you agree. But you may be thinking, "Sure, but I don't make enough to save anything." Stop that right now. Never say that again. Instead say, "I choose to spend my money on other things." People tell me they don't have any money and they grab fast-food for lunch every day. Or they buy coffee at Starbucks. Or they get their nails done. Please. You could have some savings, but you'd rather have fries. Stop lying to yourself.

Saving money is simple—you either need to earn more or spend less. I'm going to give you ideas for both. But first you must agree to do the work. You'll have to practice discipline—stop buying stuff because you want it or you're bored or your friends all have it. You'll be surprised how much money slips through your fingers. So get ready—you are going to the Pink Prepper School of Prosperity.

- 11 -

SIX STEPS TO MONEY MANAGEMENT

Step One: Fix Your Relationship with Money

I like money. Money gives me freedom (I have my own business and get to do work I love). It lets me travel and see the world. It keeps me healthy by paying for my doctors' visits and workout gear. It helps me grow by paying for conferences and books. It can help you care for your family, give to charitable causes, and help others.

Money is not evil. Money is neutral—it's a resource, a tool. You have to welcome money into your life and take care of it. If you believe it's bad and are uncomfortable making it, you'll have problems with money all your life. I say, "Yay for money!"

Most people learn about money from people who don't know anything about it. It might be your parents or your friends or Google. If your parents are wealthy and savvy with their money, this might have created a strong foundation for you (thanks, Dad). But if they were in debt up to their eyeballs, chances are they passed on some bad habits to you.

And your friends? Same deal. If they are doing well and manage their money wisely, listen to what they have to say. Don't take financial advice from people who don't have money. The best practice is to educate yourself. Read, research, and talk with trusted advisors. Reading this book is a step in the right direction.

Here are some beliefs you might have that hurt your relationship with money:

- People who care about money are evil.
- It's rude to talk about money.
- People who don't have money are honorable.
- People who inherit money are slackers.
- I don't like to think about money.
- If I have lots of money or nice things, people will think I'm uppity.
- I don't deserve to earn more money.
- My husband/partner is better with money than I am.
- Women don't manage the money in their homes.

And so on. Insert the word *hammers* for money in the statements above and you'll see how emotional/screwed up some of our beliefs about money are. Take a few minutes and consider what beliefs impact your relationship with money. I bet you hold some you don't even realize.

A 2014/2015 study by Prudential found that only 20 percent of women feel very prepared to make wise financial decisions. That means 80 percent feel they are not very prepared to make financial decisions. All of us will have to make financial decisions at some point in our lives, and we must be prepared to do so. Pink Prepper, keep reminding yourself that money is a resource to help you be prepared for life's worst. If you are smart enough to do basic math, you are smart enough to make financial decisions.

Step Two: Understand Your Money

Time to take off your pink-colored glasses. You need to know where you stand. If you are single and don't have financial software, you need to get some. I use Quicken, but it's not free, and I want you to save money. You can always upgrade to it later if you need something with more features. I recommend Mint as a free tool. If you don't want to use an app, you can use good old pen and paper or an Excel spreadsheet.

If you are married and your spouse has been managing the money, get him to walk you through everything. If he's not using some type of app or software, then encourage him to do so. It makes everything easier and you can both review and understand your finances. What do you need to know?

Assets are the fun part—they have economic value. These are assets:

- Any cash on hand, balances in checking, savings, CDs and money market accounts
- If there is a cash value for any life insurance policies
- Any investments you hold—stocks, bonds, gold, cryptocurrency
- Property—home, vehicles, boats, stuff (I wouldn't go into jewelry and art here unless you have extensive valuable collections. Even then, your fabulous artwork is only worth what someone is willing to pay for it. The man who bought my house offered me some artwork as part of payment. I was not interested, so the art was of no value in the transaction.)

You need to know the value of all your assets. Then you need to know about all the **liabilities**—all the money you owe:

- Credit card balances
- Student loan balances
- Mortgage amount
- Vehicle loans
- Any other loans—against retirement accounts, against life insurance policies, from Aunt Sue, or your beloved's bookie
- Unpaid bills

If you are single, this is easy. If you are married, you must have complete openness from your spouse. I'm hoping you already have that (and you got it before you got married), but if not, we start from where you are. You must find out your current financial position. Depending on local laws you may or may not be liable for your spouse's debt. And you may or may not be entitled to half of the assets. You need to know the laws on this one, prepper.

Why am I asking you to do all this work? To have these uncomfortable conversations? Because if you don't have this information, you cannot be prepared for much of anything. If you don't know these numbers, you don't know if you can support a child or send one to college. You don't know if you could weather a financial storm or if you are one missed paycheck away from having your car repossessed. If you and your spouse owe thousands in credit card debt and are making minimum payments, it will cost you a fortune. You need to understand this.

Bankrate.com (one of my favorite financial websites) has a credit card calculator. Let's say you owe $2,500 with a 15 percent APR and the minimum payment each month is 2 percent of the balance (these are industry averages as of this writing). You'll pay about $50 a month and will pay the balance off in 239 months (almost twenty years) and pay $3,350.95 in interest. You will pay a total of $5,850.95 for the $2,500 loan. The only one getting rich here is the credit card company.

You should know the numbers for all loans you have. Often people buy cars, furniture, or other expensive items because they can make the monthly payment. That is a fool's game.

I hear people who should know better make statements like, "I traded in my vehicle and got a new one for the same monthly payment. What a deal!" That is one stupid statement—they don't understand money. Let's say you are driving a perfectly fine car that you've had for five years. Your car payment has been $566 for all those years. In two more months, you will have the car paid off—free and clear. No car payment. Your car would go from being a liability to an asset.

You could probably drive it for five more years. But no, you want something new. So you get a new car, trade in the old one (getting nothing for it, they had to use it to get your payment to $566) and think you got a deal. New car, same payment. Yay!

No, no, no. If you kept driving your old car for those five additional years, you would have saved $32,828 ($566 x 12 months x 5 years - $1,132 (the two remaining payments on your existing car) = $32,828). And that's not counting any interest/earnings you could have made if you invested that money. Always having a car payment is not a thing. It's stupid.

Don't assume your spouse knows/understands all this. Some men talk as though they understand money, but you may be hearing from their egos, not their brains. Do the work. Trust but verify. If something happens to him, you'll be able to take care of the finances. If he's doing a bad job, you can give him some learnin'.

Hopefully after going through all this, you'll think, "Wow, we're rich!"

not, "Holy poorhouse, Batman!" Since most Americans cannot easily handle a $400 unexpected expense, the picture may not be as rosy as you hoped. Hope and ignorance are not Pink Prepper tactics. Knowledge is.

Consider the credit card example. If you didn't know how minimum payments worked before, now you know they are for suckers. Keeping your head in the sand is for losers. You are way too smart for that.

Pink Prep Principle: Minimum payments are for suckers. And monthly payments are irrelevant. Always run the numbers.

Step Three: Track Your Spending

Your assets less your liabilities equal your **net worth**—where you are financially at any given moment. Now we need to know where you are heading (or how you got where you are). Most people get paid and if they have money left in their account, they spend it (living paycheck to paycheck). They may have some retirement money automatically taken out of their paychecks, but they don't pay much attention to their spending. That is like getting in your car and randomly driving around until you run out of gas. You have no plan and no idea where you're going. You'll probably end up in the middle of nowhere with no snacks. And really, who wants that?

To get clarity, track all your spending for a month. If your beloved gets $20 out of the ATM, you need to log where he spent every penny. Tell him what you're doing and why—it's no secret. You are planning for your amazing future and to keep your family safe and prepared. If you use debit cards for everything, you can look back and use past months to analyze your spending. We're doing this for two reasons: (1) to know how much you need to live, and (2) to identify areas where you can save.

So track everything. There are two types of expenses—**fixed** (they are the same every month, like rent) and **variable** (they change every month, like your electric bill or groceries). It may also help to break out essential and nonessential expenses. Mint and Quicken can help you track these or you can go old school and use Excel or pen and paper.

COMMON EXPENSES

Rent or mortgage payments

Cell phone

Electricity, water, natural gas, trash pickup, internet, cable (utilities)

Netflix, Hulu, Amazon Prime, streaming services

Food (groceries and delivery or eating out) I would track these separately. Eating out can cost way more than you think.

Car payment

Gasoline

Car repair

Parking, tolls, vehicle registration

Clothing

Healthcare

Personal care—toiletries, make-up, hair, nails

Cleaning, paper products

Gym membership

Toys and items for children

Childcare

Insurance—auto, home, life

Health insurance

Retirement contribution

Student and other loan payments

Leisure activities

Gifts

Miscellaneous (anything that doesn't fit anywhere else)

A friend who was struggling financially asked me for help. I asked her to put together a rough estimate of her monthly expenses. Then I asked for her monthly income. I did the math and said, "Well, you're spending more than you make and you forgot to include food" (for her and her three children). We never discussed it again.

The situation was too overwhelming and hard for her to deal with. Her pretty head was buried in the sand, and her financial position continued to deteriorate. Pretending money problems aren't happening or that they will magically get better is irresponsible at best. You, dear Pink Prepper, will keep your eyes wide open and sand-free.

You may say, "But, Denise, how can I avoid that fate?"

You will make the hard choices that are ultimately better for everyone. Cora Lee, is a shining example. She worked a $6/hour job and raised Tim mostly as a single parent (another cheating husband story, sorry, prepper). Cora Lee worked hard, and little Timmy had no idea he wasn't as rich as everybody else. She lived well below her means and still managed to get him a car when he turned sixteen. Was it a new BMW? No. Did he have to pay for some of it? Yes. Cora taught him several lessons:

- You work hard and save money.
- You live below your means.
- You are not getting everything you want, you are getting what you need.
- You may not like me every day, but you will respect me.

My mom was the same. She worked hard to give me a good life, but if I wanted to go on the senior class trip, I had to get a job and pay for it. Sometimes the answer was no.

Most people say the one thing they wish their parents had done was teach them about money. Well, you must understand money before you can teach others. And right or wrong, you are teaching your kids about money every day. You might be teaching them right now that

- Mommies don't know anything about money.
- You can have anything you want.
- Keeping up with the Joneses is important.
- Mommy's future doesn't matter.
- Money falls from the sky.
- Pitching a fit gets you what you want.

Stop immediately. That's not you anymore. You are going to take a hard look at your spending and will not stop looking until you are out of debt and have an emergency fund. Vigilance now partnered with discipline will help you create the life you want and be ready for anything.

This is what you are going to teach your kids:

- Mommies are smart about money.
- You can have anything you want if you are willing to work hard and save for it.
- Keeping up with the Joneses is ridiculous.
- Mommy's future is as important as yours. And she loves you so much, she doesn't want to be a burden to you.
- Money is hard to get and should be treated with respect.
- Pitch a fit and your parents will ignore you. Terrorism will not work in our household. And we don't care what you post about us on social media.

Teach your kids about money and lead by example. They are always watching. If you aren't frugal, they won't be either. If you use credit cards as your bank, they will too. Walk your talk. My dad would always buy me any book I wanted. Not any toy, not any outfit, only any book. I have a lifetime love of books and learning to this day. Actions always speak louder than words.

Pink Prep Principle: I will be smart about money and I will teach my children to be smart about it too.

Step Four: Spend Less

Now that you have a clear picture of your current financial situation, we can work on improving it. There are two ways to do this: make more money or spend less money. Let's start with spend less money. Now that you know what you spend, you can identify areas for saving.

Jessie and Joey let me go through all their spending for the past year so I could see what was happening. We found a few simple habits were costing them a lot more than they realized. Jessie would shop at Marshalls twice a month and spend about $50 each time. Joey had gotten into the habit of stopping at a convenience store to get an energy drink and a snack both before and after work (about $10 each way). That all added up to over $500 a month.

It's those recurring small charges that add up and surprise you. Lunch out every day? Starbucks every morning? In-app purchases? Netflix? Individually, they don't seem like a big deal, but they add up.

Anything you don't see and decide on every month can be dangerous. So many payments are automated now, people forget about them. It's easy to set up payments online or pay with the swipe of a thumb; the money doesn't even seem real. This creates a disconnect with your money. Some apps have monthly fees and you may not even use them that much. But the amount seems so small. No, no, no. This is your money and it is precious.

Examine these areas closely for savings:

Any recurring payments. Can you get rid of them completely? If you have a bank account with any monthly fees, you need to get another account. There is no reason to pay monthly fees—open a free checking account. I've seen banking fees from $5 to $30 a month. Even if only $5, that's $60 a year. Switch accounts or banks. Most people can qualify to join a credit union and they often have lower fees. Do your homework.

Look at other recurring bills. Can you lower them? Rent is what it is, but maybe you can reduce your water or electricity use. Bump the air conditioning a couple of degrees higher or the heat a bit lower. Turn the lights off when you leave a room. Don't let the water run while brushing your teeth. You'll save money and the planet.

Never pay late fees. NEVER. There is no excuse for this. That is money you are throwing away. Set up autopay or stay on top of the payments. If something happens and you do get a late charge or an overdraft, always call and see if you can get it removed. Most companies will do it once for you. Get it together going forward.

Stop ordering food, eating out, and going to Starbucks as much. Let's say you go by Starbucks five days a week and spend an average of $6 each time. You eat lunch out three times a week at $15 and have food delivered twice a week for $25 (low when you consider tip). That is $125 a week, $500 a month. That's a lot of money. I'm not saying never do these things. I'm saying if you're looking for areas to save, this might provide some. These are luxuries, not necessities.

Remove temptation. Get sale alerts out of your inbox and off your phone. Bath & Body Works owned me with their constant sale alerts and coupons. There were always shiny new fragrances and packaging—whee! I finally unsubscribed. I have enough wallflower refills and candles to last a lifetime. Look for me on an episode of *Hoarders*.

These companies are masters of consumer manipulation. Give them access to your phone or your email, and they will sell you stuff. If you're trying to save, take the access away. They are better at this than you are—cut them off.

Stop spoiling your pets and your kids. I spend a small fortune on my pets. Their food, their toys, their beds, their vet bills. I bet some of you are spending a fortune on your kids. It should go without saying that if you can't pay your current bills, you should not get a pet or have a child. If you do have pets or children, you must pay for their necessities, but they don't have to have everything. This might be an area in which you can cut back.

You did not save $X on your shopping trip today. I hate it when they say at checkout, "You saved $25 today." No, I spent $139 dollars today. I would have saved money if I stayed home. Sometimes we think because we got a deal on something, we saved money. You only saved money if the purchase was something you were going to buy regardless, and the price was lower than any other as easily available.

Don't automatically ignore offers. I get a $25 annual statement credit from the electric company by allowing them to reduce my power usage during peak periods. I can tell zero difference in my power. And did I mention it was an annual statement credit? I've been doing this for over fifteen years, that's $375 dollars I've saved. My beloved was convinced we would tell a difference and was against this (but I did it anyway and he's never noticed).

Beware the sale. I've been sucked into so many sales. I have purchased far too many items of clothing I thought I'd wear. If only I could have all that money back. Know thyself—if you've made poor sale purchases like I have, step away from the discount. Often items are on sale for a reason.

Don't boredom shop. I'm guilty of this. I watch TV and check out all my favorite sites—there's usually something I want. Key word is *want*, not need. Now that I'm bringing in less money, I'm not shopping at all. It's amazing how much less I'm spending. You may do this with your friends—shopping is fun. No, shopping is expensive. Fill up that time with something else.

Review your bills. Can you increase deductibles on your home and car insurance? Take time to review them. Can you renegotiate your internet or cell phone bill? You can often get a bill lowered with a phone call.

Hair and nails. Can you wait longer between appointments or do your own nails? Use Groupons? Ask for gift cards for services for your birthday? Apply your amazing creativity to saving money.

Careful with Costco (or other discount clubs). There is some amazing stuff in Costco and Sam's Club. And everything is big and shiny and exciting! But if you throw half of what you bought away, you lost money. Compare prices always—don't assume bigger is always cheaper.

Drive your car longer. I drive my cars until the cost of repairing them exceeds their value. Cars today last a long time. Taking care of your car will save you money in the long run.

Keep your phone longer. Cell phones are expensive. Buying the latest technology to seem cool is stupid. Make sure you want to spend $699 for some minor tweaks. It doesn't seem that expensive because of the way the phone companies spread out the payments. As I write this, I have an iPhone 8. The iPhone 12 is out. By not upgrading every year (and I'm not upgrading this year), I've saved around $2,500. I also don't get insurance on my phone. I simply take care of it, saving another $6.50 a month ($78 a year). If you upgrade and get the insurance every year, you'll spend $3,000 more than I will. You be cool, I'll be rich.

Stop with the DoorDash already. Unless you are making big cash money, having restaurant food delivered multiple times a week is nuts. This should be the exception, not the rule. If you have a fully funded emergency fund, are debt-free, and are living below your means, then dash away.

Never get an extended warranty. Or a parts warranty because 99.99 percent of these are a rip-off. My beloved was buying a new washer and dryer, and the salesman was trying to talk him into getting the extended warranty (for three years for $389). I said, "Don't do it." He wasn't sure. I said, "Pay me the $389, and I'll pay for anything that happens in the next three years."

He didn't pay me, but he also didn't buy the warranty. We've had the washer and dryer for eight years with no problems. Warranties are designed to make more money for those who issue them. Do your research, buy quality items. Usually a manufacturer's warranty will cover you if there are problems. If you want to give away your money, at least read the small print on any warranty you're offered. You might be surprised at what that extended warranty is not going to cover.

There are plenty of ideas for saving money—the big takeaway is to pay attention and not spend everything that you earn. Money can easily slip through your fingers. It's much easier to spend money than to get it.

Pink Prep Principle: No spending on autopilot. Stay vigilant.

Step Five: Make More (Honey, You Need Your Own Money)

You can only do so much by saving money. I want you to make money. The way I see it, either you are working (or looking for work) or you are dependent on your spouse. If you are dependent on your spouse, you should either have a side gig that brings in money or ask for an allowance. Why not?

There is a high value in staying home and caring for children and you deserve some compensation for that. You also shouldn't be put in the position of having to ask your spouse for $5 if you want to buy a candy bar.

Don't want to be a kept woman? Honey, unless you are earning some money, you *are* a kept woman. I'm not saying that raising kids isn't hard. I'm not saying you aren't smart or capable or anything else. I'm pointing out the fact that you don't have any money coming in. (If you are independently wealthy, congratulations! This doesn't apply to you.) Every woman needs some money that is her own. Grandma called it pin money or egg money (on the farm), and the bills and coins were sitting in the sugar bowl on the top shelf in the kitchen.

Don't want to ask for an allowance? Maybe you need to join the gig economy. There are tons of opportunities out there. Maybe you're artsy and could create something to sell on Etsy. Maybe you love kids and wouldn't mind babysitting. Maybe you want to get out of the house and drive a few afternoons for Uber. Check out Fiverr.com and FancyHands.com to get other side gig ideas.

I know you have skills—put them to use. The gig economy gives you plenty of options. Love animals? Pet sit, dog walk. If you live in a neighborhood on Nextdoor.com, you could offer to run errands for your neighbors. Jessie does photography on the weekends (in addition to her full-time job). You could be a tour guide if you live in a tourist area. You are only limited by your imagination and your willingness to work.

According to the US Bureau of Labor Statistics, 72.3 percent of mothers with children under the age of eighteen work, so most of you are already bringing in some money. For you, my advice is get more money. You can do this in many ways. If you know you do excellent work and haven't gotten a pay increase in a while, *ask for a raise*. If you don't ask, you probably won't get. You can do it nicely and the worst that will happen is they'll say no.

Most women don't ask for what they are worth. We know we are worth as much as men (if not more) and we get 80 cents to their $1. Time to ask for more. If you work for yourself, consider raising your rates. You can always lower them if the market pushes back.

Work more. Maybe you can get more hours. Maybe you can add a side gig. Maybe you have a hobby you can monetize or a skill you can teach.

Get a higher paying job. You might have to start by getting better. Get some additional training so you are always increasing your value. Also keep looking. There might be a fantastic opportunity out there you don't even know about. Maybe you need to work someplace where there are more opportunities to advance. Let's face it, there are some companies where someone has to die for you to get a promotion. It might be better to look for another company.

Sell stuff. I'll be the first to admit I have made many buying mistakes. My closet has tons of shoes for the life I think I have, not the life I actually do have. (Apparently, I think I'm going out clubbing when what I'm doing is sitting home watching Netflix.)

So every time I clean out my closet, I list a few items on Poshmark. Poshmark has been the best site for me—easy to use and they don't take as big a cut as some of the other sites. Garage sales are too much work and you get rock-bottom dollar. Furniture and exercise equipment—I list on Craigslist, but Facebook Marketplace is coming on strong. I sold my childhood *Star Wars* collection on eBay—it's best for collectibles. My neighbors sell stuff on Nextdoor, but why offer something to fewer than a hundred people when you can reach thousands? But hey—you do you. Just get some money, honey.

A misleading commercial featured a woman saying she had made $30,000 selling on Poshmark. Unless those clothes grew on a tree in her backyard, she isn't making any money on Poshmark. I paid more than I made for every item I've sold. It would have been far wiser for me not to buy those items in the first place. You might be able to find an item at a flea market and sell it for more, but you could probably find a better use of your time. These sites are only a way to claw back a portion of the money you've already spent.

Pink Prep Principle: No one owes you a living. Get your hustle on. The best job security is being awesome.

Step Six: Actively Manage Your Money

Once you have some money, you need to manage it. If you're managing the household money—fantastic! If not, you may only be managing your money. That's what we do.. Tim manages his money and I manage mine. I keep up with all our joint expenses and tell him how much he owes each month. If he wants to spend his money on a crazy thing, that's his deal. Ditto for me.

I'm not saying this is the way everyone should handle their money. You should do what works for you. But I want you to always know the financial situation of your household and have some of your own money. Pink Prepper, if you do nothing else, do this.

Most financial advisors will tell you at this point to create a budget. If you already live well below your means, you don't need this. I don't have a budget; I've always earned more than I've spent. But you may find it helpful. A budget is basically a spending plan. This is where you take all those expenses you tracked in step three and put them together with your income.

Here's a simple example:

HOME BUDGET TEMPLATE

Monthly income for the month of: _____

ITEM	AMOUNT
Salary	
Spouse's salary	
Dividends	
Interest	
Reimbursements	
Other	
TOTAL	

Monthly expenses for the month of: _____

ITEM	AMOUNT
Mortgage/Rent	
Car loan	
Car insurance	
House insurance	
Life insurance	
Childcare	
Charity	
Gas/Electricity	

Telephone	
Cable	
Internet	
Food	
Pet supplies	
Healthcare	
Entertainment	
Gifts	
Clothing	
Other	
TOTAL	

Income vs. Expenses

ITEM	AMOUNT
Monthly income	
Monthly expenses	
DIFFERENCE	

Plug in what you've been earning and what you've been spending and see where you stand. Make adjustments where needed. You can set all of this up in Mint.com or other apps/software. Then during the month, you track your spending and manage accordingly.

For example, let's say you budgeted $350 for food for the month and you've already spent $300. On the twenty-fifth day of the month, your beloved takes a group of guys out to lunch and blows $50. He's on ramen for the next few days. Or you'll have to cut elsewhere. A budget is designed to help you plan your spending. It's a way to help you be strategic about your money.

Pink Prep Principle: Be strategic in your spending to be prepared for the unexpected.

In steps four and five, I gave you tips for freeing up some money. Why? I want you to set up an emergency fund.

You may feel you don't need an emergency fund. But what if you or your spouse lost a job? Or one of you was in an accident and unable to work? Or your child had to go to the emergency room, and you were hit with a big medical bill? You need to make your emergency fund a priority. Having an emergency fund is the single most important prep you can make.

You can also put any unexpected windfall in here. Your tax refund or stimulus check or if you sell something online. Maybe instead of a birthday gift, you ask your relatives to give to your emergency fund.

How large should the fund be? You need to do you, but I recommend at least three months of expenses. You should now have an idea of what it costs for you to live each month. If that's $3,000, your emergency fund should be $9,000. That will buy you time to find another job or get unemployment. I have a much larger emergency fund because that's how I roll. And I'm exceedingly glad. It allowed me to write this book and not panic with the overnight collapse of my business. It's allowing me to throw out a big fat pink life preserver to you.

I don't want you to ever be in a situation you can't get yourself out of. That's what an emergency fund is—a life preserver. It allows you to handle the stuff you can't see coming and not drown.

Pink Prep Principle: I will build an emergency fund. No excuses.

Let's talk about debt. Personally, I hate debt. It's a belief passed down from my father who lived through the Great Depression. And right now, I'm delighted I hold that belief. Everything I have from my house to my car is paid off, making my sudden drop in income easier. You don't have to live debt-free. You just have to understand debt and its impact on your finances.

According to Experian, the average American consumer had debt of $90,460 in 2018. However, this doesn't tell us much. This could be a person with a home mortgage or someone living in their parent's basement having racked up $90,000 in credit card debt. Some people have no debt and some have a lot. All that matters for you is you. If you have no debt, I applaud you and you can move to the next section. (Do be careful about taking on any debt.) If you have debt, we need to get you to work paying it off.

Should you fund the emergency fund or pay off debt? Well, my answer has to be "it depends." You must make at least the minimum payments on all your debts. If you have some crazy 20 percent interest payday lender loan, I want to see that thing gone as soon as possible. But if you have loans at a typical interest rate, I'm going to want you to make the minimum payment and start building that emergency fund. Why? So you can be prepared.

Let's say you currently have a $15,000 car loan at 5 percent interest. Your monthly payments are $283. You have no emergency fund and live paycheck to paycheck. You get a raise and have an extra $200 a month. Yay! Emergency fund or car loan?

I say emergency fund. Because if your company goes bust a year later, you'll have $2,400 to help bridge the gap. You'll need cash to pay the utilities, for food, and everything else. If you don't lose your job, but your spouse leaves you, you'll have $2,400 to help cover expenses until you can find a roommate. There are dozens of scenarios where that money would help you be prepared. Are you with me, Pink Prepper?

Everyone's situation is different, but my goal is to help you be ready for the unexpected. Having extra money is the best way to be prepared. The more money you have, the more prepared you are.

However, I don't want you to make this trade-off forever. Set up an emergency fund for three months of expenses (possibly more if your job is not secure). Then work on your debt. (If you are debt-free, skip to the next section.) Finance guru Dave Ramsey will tell you to pay off the debt with the smallest balance, so you'll feel a sense of accomplishment. If you need that, rock on. Me, I'd advise you to tackle the one with the highest rate of interest. If you owe $6,000 at 17 percent on one credit card and $2,000 at 2 percent on another, I say pay off the one with the higher interest rate.

Why? I ran some numbers assuming you have to make the minimum payment on each card (interest plus 1 percent of the balance), but you have an extra $250 to apply to either. If you apply the $250 to the $2,000, in eight months it will be paid off and you will have saved $207.83 in interest (versus paying the minimum until paid off in 137 months).

If you instead apply the $250 to the $6,000, it will take longer to pay it off (eighteen months if you keep paying the extra $250), but you'll save $3,139.08 if you pay the extra $250 *for only eight months.* Do you want to feel a win or save three grand? Pay off the higher interest rate loans first.

Here are the calculations if you don't believe me:

Loans	$2,000 at 2%	$6,000 at 17%
Minimum payment (fixed for calculations)	$23.33	$145
If only minimum made	137 months to pay off, $221.85 interest	289 months to pay off, $7,940.92 interest
Increase payment by $250 (with fixed min. payment)	8 months to pay off, $14.02 interest	18 months to pay off, $804.50 interest
After eight months	No balance	Balance of $3,393.49
	Saved $207.83 in interest	Saved $3,139.08 (over life of loan)

All that said (whew) if you prefer to pay off the smaller balance first—go for it. But don't do it blindly. As a Pink Prepper, you make smart financial decisions. Online calculators like the ones at Bankrate.com are there to help.

There are different schools of thought about debt. I hate debt because my father hates debt. And I have to say, right now with COVID-19 shutting down my business, I'm delighted not to have a car or house payment. Have I had those payments in the past? Yes, when I bought my first home, for a while I had payments. But I started with a small and affordable townhome. I made a large down payment, got a low interest rate, and set to paying that bad boy off. Could I have bought a bigger house? Yep. Could I have driven a more expensive car? Yep.

But I'm a Pink Prepper. It's more important to me to be prepared. Don't get me wrong, I still had fun during this time. I took a month-long trip to Australia and New Zealand, ate out with friends, shopped. I just didn't do those things all the time. I lived within my means. Believing you deserve something doesn't mean you can afford it.

Pink Prep Principle: What you deserve is irrelevant; buy only what you can afford.

Student loan debt is an excellent example of this. When I was looking at colleges, I was accepted by Duke University. But it was insanely expensive. I was also accepted by the University of South Carolina where I was awarded scholarships and attended the Honor's College. I couldn't afford Duke, so I didn't go there. I don't know why parents would encourage their children to take out huge loans for sometimes irrelevant degrees. Or maybe the parents are spending their own retirement money. These are bad, bad decisions and an entire generation is paying for them.

You might argue that an MBA from USC is not as good as an MBA from Duke, but I'm willing to bet that my net worth is higher than that of several of my peers who graduated from Duke. Going to an expensive school doesn't guarantee you a high-paying job, but it could put you in debt for the rest of your life. Ask some GenXers still paying off college loans how they feel about that burden.

Education is a door opener. It helps you grow and exposes you to new ideas. You should get the best education you can afford. But conduct a serious cost/benefit analysis before pursuing a degree so expensive you will be in debt for the next twenty years.

You should do this before any major purchase. What's a major purchase? That depends on your finances. If $400 would break you, $100 might be a major purchase. For someone doing well, $5,000 might be a major purchase. Make major purchases with care. Some people will drive miles to buy the cheapest gas and then buy a new car because the payments are the same as they were for the old one. They saved $2, but lost $32,000. Way to go.

Pink Prep Principle: Make no major purchase without doing your homework. If you don't research and understand something, do not buy it.

- 12 -

ADDITIONAL FINANCIAL TIPS

To be prepared for an uncertain future, you need an emergency fund. You also need a stash of cash. How large a stash is based on your lifestyle. Why cash? Let's say the power grid goes out. I saw a man selling toilet paper and hand sanitizer on the side of the road during the pandemic. He wasn't taking credit cards. Never a bad idea to have some cash.

Consider gold. My dad is always after me to buy some gold. This is not so much for investment purposes but to use if society goes completely to hell. My dad's favorite scenario: Imagine there are only ten seats on the last helicopter out of the war zone. Everyone wants on. You have five gold Krugerrands. Someone has a credit card, another a fistful of cash. Who's getting on that helicopter?

I thought he was nuts until the global pandemic and rioting. Then I thought, "Maybe I need a Krugerrand or two." This is way down my to-do list, but having gold seemed brilliant when the stock market took a nose dive. You do you, but I might add a couple gold coins to my holdings.

Consider other items. I am planning to stockpile toilet paper and hand sanitizer going forward. I was lucky to have a large stash entering the pandemic, so this was never a problem for me (hoarder that I am). For about eight months, stores had problems keeping paper products in stock. If you have a supply when the next crisis hits, it could be as good as cash (or better).

If SHTF, what we consider money might change. Since all the social unrest in the US, the price of ammunition has skyrocketed and there are shortages in supply. Ammo might be worth more than gold (and easier to barter with) if supply chains collapsed. Thoughts like this seemed crazy in January 2020. Now, not so much.

Credit card debt is your arch enemy because the interest rates are so high. As of this writing, the average credit card charges over 16 percent interest. You know how much you get in a money market account? .08 percent. Carrying a balance on a credit card is financially disastrous. Pay them off.

The less debt you have, the more prepared for uncertainty you are. I know plenty of people who were flying high, renting out second homes on VRBO—and then wham! Try making two house payments when you lost your job and there's a travel ban. I'm not saying don't do this, I'm saying don't do this if you can't afford an unforeseen downturn.

Don't take advice from idiots. If someone has less money than you, they have no credibility regarding finance. If they have a history of making bad financial decisions, they have no credibility. If they are some random person on Facebook or a friend's cousin, they have no credibility.

For example, Jessie's hubby told her, "You don't have to pay medical bills, just let them go to collections." (He used this genius strategy himself when he was young, and they had since fallen off his credit report.) So she thought, "Yay, free money!" As soon as I heard this, I said that was insane and she needed to pay her bills. She paid the bill, but it had already gone to collection. When they went to buy a home, she couldn't qualify for a loan because her credit was bad. Do not let bills go to collection.

Creditors will often work with you if you call them. They will work out payment plans. Believe me, they don't want to send your bill to collection—they want the money. Don't ignore them—work with them. You're a responsible adult and you can handle this.

Always do your own homework. If something seems too good to be true, it probably is. A rule you learn in business school is TANSTAAFL—there ain't no such thing as a free lunch. This is a rule to apply in business and life in general. If you think, "Duh, everyone knows that," I have another two words for you—Bernie Madoff.

Get the insurance you need. In most states, if you want to drive, you must have auto insurance. If you have children or other dependents, you should probably have life insurance. If you are renting an apartment and have possessions you can't afford to replace, you need renter's insurance. If you own your own home, you need homeowner's insurance. Everyone should have some form of health insurance. This is an area you need to do your homework in. The type of coverage you need is a complicated question, and there are many options.

I have high deductibles on my car and home insurance because I can afford to pay them, and I'd rather lower my insurance bill. I might have an accident, but I'll definitely have an insurance bill. You may not be comfortable with this option. I don't have kids, so I don't have life insurance. My estate will leave enough to pay for my funeral. When I rented, I had renter's insurance. You should too. It's affordable and if the blockhead above you leaves a candle burning and sets the whole building on fire, you'll be able to replace everything. The insurance company will probably pay for your hotel while you look for a new place to live.

Talk to someone you know and trust who is savvy about the topic before you talk with an insurance agent. Or do your own research and homework. Some agents are outstanding and will help you; others only want to sell insurance—that's how they get paid. I also have liability insurance for my business and an umbrella policy to cover me beyond the limits of my other insurance.

There is also disability and long-term care insurance, pet insurance, dental insurance, eye care insurance, and who knows what other kinds of insurance. (You already know how I feel about cell phone insurance.) Never buy anything you don't fully understand.

And get multiple quotes. The variance in what companies charge is shocking. Sometimes you can save money by writing multiple policies with the same company, but make sure the company is solid. Look at reviews online (Bankrate.com comes through again).

Review all your statements regularly. Thomas got his car insurance statement and the amount had dramatically increased. He could have concluded it was time for a rate increase (or maybe not even noticed it, it was on autopay). But he took the time to call his insurance company. They said it was because of the speeding ticket he had gotten. Only problem—he hadn't gotten any speeding tickets.

He had to do some digging. First to the company that reports to the insurance company. They gave him the date of the supposed ticket. He was in Vegas that day, not North Carolina where the ticket was issued. He then contacted the DMV, got a copy of his driving record, and there it was. He called them back, explained the situation, they researched it and found out it was a mix-up. They put someone else's speeding ticket on his driving record!

That could have been a huge deal—not only with increased insurance premiums for years, but if he were to get a ticket, he might get harsher penalties. I've had fraudulent charges on my credit cards and refunds never issued. Reviewing your statements is important.

Pink Prep Principle: No one is going to take better care of your money than you.

- 13 -

MORE FINANCIAL RISKS

Now that your financial house is in order and you prepped (or are prepping) for an unexpected financial hardship, you need to have some other financial risks on your radar. You probably will want or need to stop working full-time at some point, so retirement isn't a maybe. It's coming and you need to be prepared. As we spend more and more time online and using technology, we are increasingly vulnerable to cybercrime. The last thing we want to do is lose the money we've worked so hard for. Read on, financial prepper.

Not Enough Money for Retirement

Women need to wake up when it comes to their retirement. Most of us don't have anywhere near enough money to retire. It's time to stop pretending, woman up, and take a cold hard look at how much you will need and make a plan to get it.

Hopefully, you looked at one of the retirement calculators I listed earlier to get a rough idea of where you are. Take time to get the numbers as close to correct as possible. It's worth sitting down and contemplating the lifestyle you want in retirement. Will you want to travel? Or stay home with the grandkids? Try to get a monthly number that seems realistic and enter the data. See what the results are.

Ignorance is not bliss. If it seems like a huge number you'll never get, don't stick your head back in the sand. Time to be woke about your situation. Maybe you can't have that freewheeling lifestyle you thought you could have in retirement. Maybe you need to stop your current carefree lifestyle and start saving. Maybe you're better off than you thought. The only thing that is unacceptable is ignorance. You're a Pink Prepper and that is not how we roll. Run the numbers, assess where you are, and start acting accordingly.

Social security is not a retirement plan. I've been paying into social security my entire life. And as of this writing (according to the Social Security Administration's own website), it's projected to run out of money in 2037. Great. That will be the year I plan to retire. GenX screwed again.

So I don't include social security when I run my scenarios. The government is printing money like it grows on trees, so counting on them to take care of your financial future is like asking an alcoholic to tend your bar.

Having no debt will help. I'll roll into retirement with no house payment, no car payment, no debt. We may even downsize and have equity from our home we could use to pay living expenses. See how beautiful being debt-free can be? You save money now (not paying interest) and don't have to worry about those payments when your income stops.

If your employer has any kind of retirement savings matching program, maximize it. If you are lucky enough to have an employer who offers a 401(k) or IRA or similar match, grab it with both hands. As a minimum, contribute the amount needed to get the full amount of the match. This is free money, Pink Prepper. Get it!

These programs vary by employer. Talk with human resources or payroll and ask questions until you understand this and every other benefit you might have. Too many people have benefits they don't fully understand and utilize. You work hard for these—make them work for you.

If you are self-employed, make saving for retirement a priority. Research the different retirement plans and figure out which one makes the most sense for you. Saving for retirement will let you keep some of your earnings from Uncle Sam, so make the most of this. Also research health savings accounts (I am a big fan of these). I make the highest possible contribution to my HSA and then pay for all my healthcare out of pocket. I plan to use that money for healthcare when I retire.

Start saving now. Preparing for retirement seems so lame when you're young. You're worried about dating and student loans and makeup and shoes, and retirement seems like an eternity from now. Here's an example to show you the light.

- Contribute $200 a month starting at age twenty-five at 5 percent interest, and when you turn sixty-five, you'll have put in $96,000 and will have $295,511.96.
- Wait until you're forty and put in $400 a month (twice as much) at 5 percent interest, and when you turn sixty-five, you'll have put in $120,000 and you'll only have $233,297.19.

- If you waited until forty, you'll put in $24,000 *more* and you'll have $62,214.77 *less*.

Start now. You will never be any younger, you can't go back. Take as much advantage of the power of compounding interest as you can. Put your money to work today making money for you tomorrow.

Have a chat with your future self. Imagine yourself at sixty-five. Do you want that woman to be able to take care of herself? To take a trip after years of working or caring for others? Or do you want her to be broke and unable to pay for care? (She will outlive her spouse.) The actions you take now determine the choices she will (or won't) have. Personally, my nightmare is having to send her to the cheapest nursing home because I didn't have the discipline to save for her.

No one cares more about your retirement than you. If you think the US government or your employer deeply cares about your retirement, well, as we say in the South, bless your heart. I'm not saying they are evil; I'm saying they are concerned with many, many other things. If you won't even take the time to figure how much you need to retire and make your future a priority, why should they? Understand and make the most of what they give you, but know only you have your back.

Don't feel overwhelmed. The problem with trying to give you a step-by-step process is that each of you is different. A married, middle-aged woman with three children is going to make different financial decisions than a recent college graduate who is single with no kids. But never underestimate how smart you are. Read books on finance, take classes, visit blogs, ask questions. Knowledge is Pink Power. If you can afford it and feel you need to, consult a financial advisor. The heavy lifting is you applying discipline to prepare for your future rather than doing what you want in the present.

Identity Theft

Not only do you have to earn and save your money, you also have to protect it from all the people out there who want to take it. You do this by making it extremely hard for them.

The chances of your identity being stolen are small, but if it happens to you, it could be a nightmare. And as more information is floating around about us online and more hackers are trying to access it, it's worth discussing.

I love my RedCard—and Target got hacked. The last thing I want to do is lose my retirement savings so I could save 5 percent at Tarzhay. We need to protect ourselves, prepper.

Identity theft is when someone does something pretending to be you. They might open a credit card in your name, rent an apartment, access your bank or retirement accounts, who knows what. You work too hard to have someone else racking up a bunch of debt in your name.

Immediately check one of your credit reports (if you haven't done so in a while) and freeze your credit. You can check your credit report for free at annualcreditreport.com. This is the *only* free credit report site authorized by the Federal Trade Commission (FTC).

The credit reporting companies have to give you a free copy of your credit report annually. If you want to keep an eye on your report, you could check Experian in January, TransUnion in May, and Equifax in September. If you see any errors, accounts you didn't open, or credit check inquiries from companies you've never heard of, RED ALERT. Contact the creditor immediately. If you see a credit check from Bass Pro Shops and you'd rather crawl through broken glass than go hunting or fishing, call the Bass Pro Shops credit card company immediately. Contact numbers are usually on the credit report.

Now, before you start saying, "I've got Credit Karma, I don't need to do all this," STOP RIGHT THERE. Remember Jessie and that medical bill she let go to collection? She was shocked it impacted her—her credit score didn't go down on Credit Karma. Get the real deal. Your credit report from the credit reporting company. If you're going for a big loan (house or car), check them all. Jessie's medical bill only showed up on one.

To freeze your credit, you'll have to go to each of the big three credit reporting companies directly (contact information is on annualcreditreport. com) and request a credit freeze. You can do this online. Now, if you are in Marshalls and they say, "If you get a Marshalls card today, you'll save 20 percent on your purchase and get 5 percent back on all future purchases," and you look at your full cart and say, "Yes!" you will have to unfreeze your credit before they can open the card.

If you want to buy a car, get a store credit card, do anything that involves a credit check, you'll need to unfreeze your credit to make that happen. The bad guys can't open a credit card in your name, but you can't either. For most of us, that's probably a good thing. Do this, my pretty.

Get a shredder. You can get a cheap one, but if you work from home or have a lot of financial documents you need to shred, you can get a workhorse for around $150. (It will last forever.) Offers for credit cards in the mail? Shred. Anything that has your social security number, your birth date, credit card numbers, account numbers, and medical insurance numbers? Shred. When in doubt, shred. I keep seven years of backup for my tax returns. When I do my taxes, I shred the earliest year of records. (Keep your returns forever.) Shredding is your friend.

Be careful what others can see or access. If you have people who come to clean or do other work in your home or office, make sure you turn off computers and put away anything that might have sensitive data on it (credit card statements, other bills). Anytime other people are in your home, protect your electronics and information.

Tim calls it "keeping honest people honest." Some people can't help themselves when opportunity presents itself. Don't present the opportunity to rip you off.

Sign up for Informed Delivery at USPS.com. Set up an account at USPS.com, the US Postal Service. You'll have to register, but this is super useful if you ever need to order stamps or ship something without going to the post office. Anyway, after you register, go to your profile and click on preferences. You'll see Informed Delivery. Set it up. You'll be able to see what's been delivered to your home for the past week. Not everything, but most of my bills were there.

If you start missing bills or your beloved gets his mail, but some of yours are missing, you can check here to try to determine what's happening. If a bill was scanned and you didn't receive it, it's possible someone took it out of your mailbox to steal your account data. Call the issuing company immediately, tell them the situation and follow their instructions. If you didn't receive a bill and it wasn't scanned, call the issuing company and verify your address. Keep a close eye on the account for any activity you didn't authorize. It's possible the bill was lost in the mail, but better safe than sorry.

Reconcile your accounts. This seems to be a bit of a lost art. When I ask young people if they reconcile their accounts, they look like I said, "Do you know what a postage meter is?" I get it—everything is electronic. They make purchases and automatically have the account balances drafted out of their checking accounts. But here's the problem. If one of the companies set up on autopay incorrectly charges them for something, they probably won't catch it. They are not paying that much attention to their money.

You can reconcile electronically or old school, but you must do it. When your monthly statement is available, review it. Match it up with all the charges you know you made. I keep all my receipts. When the statement is available, I go through and match up all the receipts with the statement.

Sometimes I'll discover I was never credited for a return or that an autopay amount made a big jump and I need to check into what's going on (a water bill goes way up and you find you have a leak). This is also how you discover that the Netflix subscription you thought you had canceled isn't canceled. Many apps and software programs offer you a free month or two and then begin monthly charges. If you're not paying attention, these can add up.

Reconciling can protect you in bigger ways. I had a small $2.99 charge on my iTunes account. No big deal, right? Well, I knew I hadn't bought anything. When I called, it turned out someone had hacked my account. Apple took care of it, but I needed to change any accounts that had the same password. Sometimes little fraudulent test charges that go unnoticed lead to larger fraudulent charges. If you don't pay attention and keep an eye on your accounts, someone else will. Review all statements and reconcile those accounts (all banking, credit cards, loans).

Destroy/swipe electronics. If you sell or donate a computer, phone, or almost any other electronic device, make sure every bit of data is removed. Don't simply delete everything and empty the trash folder. Norton.com has a good article on how to thoroughly wipe a hard drive. Consider this for any electronic item you want to get rid of. I destroyed my old Fitbit. I don't want any information about me to be available to bad guys (and I'd prefer no one know my weight).

But have you thought about your car? Modern cars collect all kinds of data about you. Make sure it's all deleted, cleared, removed before the car belongs to someone else. Reset the garage door opener if you have a program like HomeLink, unpair your phone, log out of the cloud account some automakers have.

Assume the worst. Don't give out personal information over the phone unless you made the call and you know you've reached your bank, insurance company, or Microsoft. If someone calls you randomly, claiming to be from one of these companies, offer to call them back. Then call the number on the company's website.

Some of these inbound calls can be scary. I got one from someone claiming to be from the IRS and immediately my heart rate increased. These are almost always bogus. Scammers know how terrified people get when someone says they are calling from the IRS. It's such a common scam, the IRS even addresses it on their website.

Another scam call I got was from someone claiming to be with Microsoft with an important technical update. Microsoft is not going to call you about your computer. This is from Microsoft's website: "Microsoft does not send unsolicited email messages or make unsolicited phone calls to request personal or financial information, or to fix your computer. Any communication with Microsoft has to be initiated by you."

Assume if some business is calling you out of the blue, it's to get your money (either to sell you something legitimately or con you).

Enter your email address into www.haveibeenpwned.com. It will let you know if your email address was involved in a data breach and, if so, on which sites. Both of my email addresses had been involved in breaches on sites I rarely use. I deleted the accounts and made sure I wasn't using the passwords anywhere else. It's concerning—there are a surprising number of breaches out there. And my personal information is in way too many places I don't want it to be. I bet yours is too.

Spend time with Google's security settings (if Google is your browser) to check your passwords. To access this, simply log into your Google account. You'll see a menu with several options. The security tab opens a screen with several options, one of which is a password manager. If you click on that, it takes you to another screen that offers a password checkup. I was impressed with what this revealed to me. It flagged seven accounts (I had long forgotten about) where I was using the same password as the one used on the breached accounts. One contained credit card info. Holy not prepping! I deleted some accounts and changed more passwords. It took time but my accounts are much more secure now.

Click no links in emails. I get weird links or odd attachments from email addresses I recognize. Typically with a somewhat off-kilter message. It's usually clear they are sketchy. But when in doubt, I contact the sender.

I bet a lot of you are thinking, "I wouldn't fall for any of this, please." Well, while I didn't fall for the IRS and Microsoft calls, they gave me pause. And if these didn't work on someone, they wouldn't keep doing them. The bad guys are working at improving their scams all the time. So we have to be more vigilant and, sadly, more skeptical, all the time too.

Be suspicious. Here's an email I recently received:

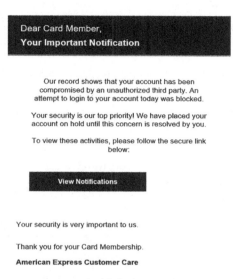

AMERICAN EXPRESS

Dear Card Member,
Your Important Notification

Our record shows that your account has been compromised by an unauthorized third party. An attempt to login to your account today was blocked.

Your security is our top priority! We have placed your account on hold until this concern is resolved by you.

To view these activities, please follow the secure link below:

View Notifications

Your security is very important to us.

Thank you for your Card Membership.

American Express Customer Care

DON'T *live life* WITHOUT IT™

PRIVACY STATEMENT | UPDATE YOUR EMAIL

Your account information is included above to help you recognize this as a customer care e-mail from American Express. © 2020 American Express. All rights reserved.

AMERICAN EXPRESS

Sneaky, eh? At first glance, looks legit. But the return address was American Express mkramer@xxxxxxx.com. If I hovered my mouse over the view notifications button, it did not show the American Express website. It was some weird link. Other red flags—no use of my name, the random exclamation mark after priority, and the mentioning of security about forty-three times, even in the small print. Nice try, scammers. Pink prevails.

Never give out personal information in response to an email. They might look super legit—logos copied, even real physical addresses at the bottom. But as in the Amex example, if you hover your cursor over the links (don't click) or the email addresses, you'll see the fake ones underneath. Most legitimate places will not ask for personal information via email. Always err on the side of caution.

Lock down your privacy settings. Start with your browser. I used Google's privacy checkup and was surprised how available my location data and other information was. To access this, log into your Google account. You'll see a tab for data and personalization. Clicking on this takes you to a page with an option to take a privacy checkup. Going through this allows you to decide if you are okay with being tracked (and thus shown more customized ads) or not. It only takes a few minutes and is a smart thing to take the time to do. This isn't about going off the grid. This is about being reasonably safe in a world that is designed to spy on you.

Amazon tracks everything you buy, everything you watch on Amazon Prime, possibly everything you say (if you have Alexa). They may have cookies enabled on your computer or phones that let them see what you do on other sites. And they are only one of the marketers engaging in these activities. Google knows way too much about all of us.

The simple truth is the less information legitimate companies have about you, the less hackers can get. Even if you trust good ol' Jeff Bezos, if Amazon gets hacked, we're all going down.

After your browser, check the privacy settings of your operating system. I have Windows 10 (just go into settings and click on privacy) and was surprised to know that Xbox has access to everything on my computer (photos, videos, search history). I use my computer to work, not play Xbox. It was even launching at startup. Go through all the tabs on the privacy screen. It's worth it.

Be careful with social media. Check your privacy settings on all the sites you use regularly. Facebook is constantly changing these and you might believe everything is locked down when it's not. The best guide is to not put anything online that you wouldn't want to see on a billboard (next to your picture). Unless it is your picture, then you need to be okay with that being on a billboard.

If you are looking for a job, most companies will check out your social media. Do you want a potential employer to see all that angsty dark stuff you posted in your teens? Or those party pics that make you look like a raging alcoholic? You may think, "No worries, my privacy settings are ironclad." Well, I was standing in line to check into a conference when one of the women at the check-in table said, "Wow! I can't believe she posted this!" She then turned her laptop around and showed the picture to all twenty of us standing there. Yeah. So much for your ironclad privacy settings.

What if you have children? Parents post pictures of their kids everywhere revealing ages, genders, where they go to school, the car they are driven in, where they live and so on. If you're not worried about yourself, worry about them. Close the electronic curtains, prepper. (Grandparents, take note. Don't post pics of those adorable grandchildren either.)

I spent fifteen minutes checking the latest Facebook privacy settings. I turned off facial recognition. (You'll find this in your Facebook settings menu.) Do I want Facebook selling that to unknown third parties? Can you imagine the implications? Is making it easier for friends to tag you in pictures more important than letting God knows who identify you across the web and in the world? If my friends want to tag me, I'm sure they can figure it out.

Review all the apps and websites you've let link to your Facebook account. You'll find them when you click on the apps and website tab in your Facebook settings menu. I disconnect all of those. Zillow does not need access to my Facebook information.

Even LinkedIn has issues. If you carefully read all the small print when you sign up for the service, it says they own the rights to all the content you post there. What? None of us is paying attention and we are agreeing to everything to get to play in the sandbox.

Spokeo = our worst nightmare. Go right now to Spokeo.com and search for yourself. Scary, huh? Now opt out. There are instructions on how to do it on the site. I've done it before and my information is back on there, so I'm planning to keep doing it on a regular basis and see if it sticks. I'd prefer no one have this information about me, much less anyone willing to pay $1.95.

Disable location services. Pick up your phone (these setting are for iPhones—they may vary for others), click on Settings. Then click on Privacy. Let's start with Location Services. Take a look at how many apps have access to your location. You do you, but I don't need Bath & Body Works to know where I am. I disabled tracking (because that's what "location services" is) on almost everything. Go back to the main privacy screen and work your way down. How about contacts? You might be surprised what apps have access to your contact list. You okay with that? If not, restrict access. If the legit companies can access this information, hackers probably can too.

Here's an example of a problem. If you click on photos during this process, you see the following message: "Photos stored on your iPhone may contain other information, such as where and when the photo was taken." So you are on vacay, happily posting photos telling the whole universe where you are. The universe that includes child predators, thieves, marketers, and your psychotic ex.

It gets worse. If I want to steal your identity, look at how much information I can get from what you blindly give me (details about your current location, your children, if a man is in your life or not, your income, how you spend your time, what shows you watch, what food you eat, what medical issues you have and on and on).

I know people who accept almost every friend request they receive (bye-bye privacy settings). And most people could be sucked into accepting a well-crafted fake profile as a friend. Always take a few minutes to examine a friend request. I've gotten requests that at first glance seemed legit, only to realize on closer examination they seemed bogus. When in doubt, lock them out. Once you accept a friend request, that person can see your whole family, pets, cars, the interior of your home. They might be able to guess passwords, see electronic devices they could hack into in photos or videos. And let's not forget about those lonely/drunk/angry posts—things you said at a vulnerable moment. Prepper, put your clothes back on.

Protect your medical insurance card like your credit cards. A rising problem is medical identity theft. Health insurance is expensive. Some people don't have it and would love to have yours. Review statements and call your insurance company immediately if you see charges you didn't make. And don't forget to reconcile. My dentist charged me $300 for a procedure. When I reviewed my statement, I saw my insurance company paid him as well. I called for my refund.

Manage your passwords. Best practice is to use a password manager. I tried one for a while and it got on my nerves. So Google has become my password manager and that's not so bad it turns out. I find it easier than the other options, so you might consider it as well. Here are some tips if you don't take what is the better route and get a password manager:

- **Change your passwords frequently.** This is to try and stay ahead of the breaches.

- **Don't use the same password on multiple sites.** Why? Well, remember the Target hack? I'm not 100% sure that's how my password was released into the wild, but my Target password was definitely obtained by hackers. If the hackers had immediately gone to some of my other accounts, they might have gotten access.

- **Make strong passwords.** *123456* and *password* are the most used passwords. Be more creative. Most sources say the best password is a long random string of numbers, letters, and symbols. Of course, none of us can remember those—thus the password manager. Ugh.

- **Keep your passwords out of your email.** If I could hack into your email, search for "password," and find something, that's no good. Try it and get rid of any passwords or links to reset passwords.

- **Set up two-step verification for all important accounts.** This means even you cannot gain access with a password alone. You also must enter a code from a text or an email or even a phone call. I have this on all my banking accounts, my medical account, my cloud backup account, and my Google account. I recommend you set it up for your Google account as well if you have one. Add it to any account you access online that you want to protect. It's an additional line of defense.

Be sneaky with answers to security questions. This genius idea is from Bart McDonough's book *Cyber Smart: Five Habits to Protect Your Family, Money, and Identity from Cyber Criminals.* When a site gives you the opportunity to set the answers for security questions like "What's your mother's maiden name?" instead of giving the real answer, give something like "Chocolate Milk." There is no way someone could get that answer from a stupid site like Spokeo and get into your account.

This also helps if you have posted everything under the sun about yourself on social media—birthday, hometown, alma mater, pet names— you get the idea. If the answers to your security questions are posted on Facebook, they aren't very secure, are they?

Look for the lock. If you are doing anything online involving money, make sure the site is secure. HTTPS not just HTTP. Usually you'll see a little lock symbol in front of the site address in the search bar. That means the site is secure. If you don't see the lock, don't give the site your credit card info. No lock, keep it in your pock(et). Those cheesy sayings are harder to come up with than you think.

Careful with what matters most. I travel a lot for work, and I don't access any of my banking or investment accounts from my mobile devices on public networks. If you have a portable VPN (virtual private network) this would be fine, but if not, better safe than sorry.

Cyber Attack

Several of the tips already given will help you avoid cyber attacks (things like ransomware, malware, and viruses). And let me warn you, before you start messing with any of your router or computer settings, do the following:

Back up your devices. I use a program that automatically backs up everything on my computer to the cloud. I chose that over an external hard drive in case of fire or flood. My business exists primarily on my computer. If you're like me, your whole life is on there. Or maybe it's on your phone. Either way, you need secure backup. Some people opt for both the external hard drive and the cloud backup. Again—do your homework and do you.

Let's say you don't have a backup and you get one of those ransomware attacks where you have to pay or they delete your hard drive. No backup? You're paying. Me? I'm not paying cyber terrorists. If you do opt for the external hard drive, disconnect it from your computer after you back up or the ransomware can infect it as well.

Important note: While writing this, I've been downloading different antivirus programs, running driver update software, changing router settings, and some of it has made me want to gouge my own eyes out. I spent four hours writing one day, uninstalled a driver update program, and crashed my computer. Four hours of writing gone.

Don't be me. Mess with this stuff when you have time and are not working on anything else. When I changed my router settings (see below), I also had problems with my printer connecting to the network. All can be resolved, and this is vitally important to do. Be ready for hiccups and be patient as you go through the process. It won't kill you and it will make you stronger.

Keep your operating system updated. Whenever you get the notice that your operating system needs to be updated, update it. There are often security updates and fixes included. Apple and Microsoft learn of a new virus; they make an update—we simply need to install it. This is true for your apps and software as well. Keep them all current or they can be vulnerable.

Use antivirus software and malware and keep it current. Make sure the antivirus program you started using back in 1990 is still top of the line. Check and see if you need to add a program like Malwarebytes (free).

Careful what you download. Games and apps are often the biggest culprits, infected with spyware and other nasty programs you do not want on your system. Remember TANSTAAFL about the free lunch? If a cool app or program is free, how do you think they make money? By loading you up with adware or farming your data. Don't let your technologically genius children download random programs onto your computer or phone. Teach them early to pay more attention.

Delete apps you no longer use. When I checked out the privacy setting on my phone, I realized some of the apps tracking me were ones I didn't even use anymore. Take some time and dump them. Being organized is a Pink Prep plus.

Lock down your router. You don't want to allow hackers into your home or let freeloaders access your Wi-Fi. I never thought about our router password. We used the long line of default gobbledygook that came with it. I thought, "It's a complicated password, it must be secure." Uh, no. Apparently, those passwords can be gotten from a simple internet search.

Set up a new unique one. In addition, experts recommend enabling WPA2 as your security standard. If your router is so old, it doesn't have WPA2, it's time to get a new router. Take a look, change the password and network name, set up automatic updates, and move on.

If you want even more detail on this, I recommend the McDonough book I mentioned earlier.

Cover your webcam. Why not? It can be hacked and how creepy is it to have someone watching you? This is even more important for your kids who may be visiting who knows what website and screen sharing with, well, who knows? Many young people are wildly naive when it comes to the internet. They believe everything that's posted regardless of the source, and they believe everyone is who they say they are. Set them straight.

We spend much of our time online now, so that's where the bad guys are spending much of their time. If you are not taking these precautions, it's like running around naked with the blinds open, the front door unlocked, and a big pile of cash in the entryway. Let's lock it down, prepper.

Refuse to be blackmailed. This is creepy. I got an email with the subject line: your password is XXXXXX (an actual password I had used on my Target account and others). I panicked and opened it immediately. It went on to say that the sender had gained access to my webcam, caught me in a compromising position, and was going to send video to all my contacts in Outlook and on Facebook. If I didn't want that to happen, I was instructed to send $1,887 to a bitcoin account.

At first, I was concerned because I recognized the password. Luckily, I no longer used it anywhere, but I had to check. Imagine if you got a random email with one of your actual passwords in the subject line. Once I calmed down, I just deleted it. But I share this message with you because hackers and scammers can get bits of real information they will try and use against you. Disturbing.

Trust no one online. We believe other people are like us. We're not spending our time creating fake online identities to trick or scam people, so we think no one else is either. The internet gives complete strangers a scary degree of access to us. Anyone can approach you online and you have absolutely no idea who they are. Look out for these red flags:

- **Anyone who wants to communicate with you off the platform.** If you are selling something on Poshmark or eBay, if someone wants you to email or text or call them and not communicate on the site, that's a red flag. They may be trying to get financial information about you. If they are legit, they'll have no problem talking with you through the site. Sometimes this happens on dating sites—if someone wants to meet up too quickly, you might want to slow that down. Sometimes people want to get off the platforms so there will no longer be a record of their activity. Trust your gut.

- **Unsolicited email that seems too good to be true.** I'm amazed by the number of speakers who were taken in by a scam going around a few years ago. A person would contact a speaker pretending to be organizing a big conference overseas. They offered a significant, but not ridiculous, speaking fee and went on to say how impressed they were with the speaker. After exchanging a few emails, the speaker would be asked to send about $500 to arrange for a visa. There was some song and dance about how it had to come directly from the speaker and would be reimbursed with all travel expenses. This worked because most speakers have big egos and thought it perfectly plausible that someone would pay a big fee to hear their amazing, life-changing message.

Seldom do completely random extraordinary offers pop in your inbox. If it sounds too good to be true, it is.

- **Duplicate Facebook friend requests.** Several of my friends have had their Facebook accounts hacked. Someone basically sets up a duplicate account, steals a few photos from the original, and starts sending out friend requests. Many people fall for this, assuming instantly this is their friend and accepting the request. There you go, giving a stranger access to all your personal data and information. And if you're a parent, you might be giving a predator access to all your children's data.

Consumer Reports has a fantastic resource (https://securityplanner. consumerreports.org) to help you create a customized data security plan. I didn't even know there were privacy settings on my Fitbit until I went through this tool. It's surprisingly in-depth and easy to use.

Pink Prep Principle: I will make it as hard to take my money as it was to earn it, and then some.

- 14 -

HEALTH PREP

Health is the foundation of everything. If you don't feel well, it impacts every aspect of your life. It is much harder to deal with the usual (much less the unexpected) when you are sick or in pain. Pink Preppers realize the importance of being as healthy as they can, so when they do get hurt or ill, they are impacted less and can recover more quickly.

With all health issues, consult your doctor before you undertake a new exercise program or diet or stop/start taking any supplements or medicines. If you don't feel comfortable talking with your doctor, you need to find a new one. Your healthcare provider should listen to you and address your concerns, not blow you off. There are some great docs out there and some not so great docs. (Dr. Google does not count.)

I'm a certified health coach, but I am not a doctor, so please talk with your doctor before making any changes recommended here.

A health issue is something you don't see coming that significantly impacts your life. Remember my arthritis story? My recovery was so much easier because I was fit going into surgery. The same would have been true if I had been in a car accident. I would be more likely to survive than someone in poorer condition.

Consider these two components to being prepared for unexpected health issues: One is taking care of our health (as we will discuss), the other is taking care of our money. If you must take time off work to recover or have medical bills, you'll need money. People who have money can afford healthcare, medicines, special treatments, whatever they need. This is an example of how prep work in one area can help in another.

Being prepared financially also helps you manage health risks. So a Pink Prepper has to take care of her health (to prepare for the unforeseen) and save money to cover potential medical expenses.

Lower Your Risks

The tips for being healthy will help you be prepared for the next pandemic. If you implement them, you will be as healthy as possible and alleviate or lessen the severity of some preexisting conditions (with COVID-19 certain preexisting conditions could cost you your life).

To be a Pink Prepper when it comes to your health, follow these guidelines:

If you smoke, you must stop that nonsense. It is killing you and it's expensive. If you are a smoker, stopping should be the first thing you do after reading this book. The average smoker smokes twelve cigarettes a day. Let's say you smoke ten. There are twenty cigarettes in a pack. So every year you smoke roughly 182 packs at about $5 a pack. That's $912 a year. You've been smoking ten years? That's almost $10,000. Not to mention all the extra health issues you might have and the associated costs of those.

According to the CDC, "Smoking leads to disease and disability and harms nearly every organ system of the body. It is the leading cause of preventable death." Stop smoking now.

You need to be fully aware of the impact of alcohol and act accordingly. New studies indicate the best policy is not to drink alcohol at all. No doctor on the planet will tell you to start drinking if you don't. A drink a day may decrease a woman's risk of heart disease but increase her risk of breast cancer.

Dariush Mozaffarian, dean of the Friedman School of Nutrition Science and Policy at Tufts University, says, "It's clear that drinking comes with health risks, and far less clear that it comes with any benefits." For years, everyone thought a glass of red wine was like medicine. Turns out, not so much.

Drinking does impact your health, but you might be willing to make the trade-off. What I'm also concerned with, my Pink Pretty, is what it does to your preparedness. As a nondrinker, I'm aware of how drunk people think they are and how they actually are. I've had to slip drunk friends out of bars because they let some guy they had no intention of going home with buy them way too many drinks. I've always been the designated driver (while my drunk passengers shouted out ridiculous driving instructions. Why are drunk people so loud?).

Alcohol impairs your judgment. You think you're sexy and hilarious when you're really just a hot mess. You get in situations you wouldn't if you were sober. You can ruin your career by drinking too much at company events (seen it happen). And worst of all, you can become a target.

Here's the bottom line: if you are under the influence of anything, you are not prepared. So choose wisely, dear prepper, and if you are going to partake outside your own home, have a sober Pink Prepper with you who can drive, call for help, and keep your face off social media. Drunk, stoned, high = vulnerable (at the very least, to your own poor decisions).

Keep up with your preventive checkups and tests. Here's what you need according to MedlinePlus.gov from the National Library of Medicine:

> **Blood pressure screening:** Have your blood pressure checked at least once every two years. If you have diabetes, heart disease, kidney problems, or certain other conditions, you may need to have your blood pressure checked more often, but at least once a year.
>
> **Cholesterol screening:** Recommended starting age for cholesterol screening is age forty-five for women with no known risk factors for coronary heart disease. It is age twenty for women with known risk factors. Women with normal cholesterol levels do not need to have the test repeated for five years. If you have diabetes, heart disease, kidney problems, or certain other conditions, you may need to be monitored more closely.
>
> **Diabetes screening:** If you are over age forty-four, you should be screened every three years. If your blood pressure is 130/80 mm Hg or above, your provider may test your blood sugar level for diabetes. If you have a body mass index (BMI) greater than 25 (23 for those of Asian descent) and have other risk factors for diabetes, you should be screened.

Dental exam: Go to the dentist once or twice every year for an exam and cleaning. Your dentist will evaluate if you need more frequent visits.

Eye exam: Have an eye exam every two years or more often if recommended by your provider. Have an eye exam at least every year if you have diabetes.

Immunizations: You should get a flu shot every year. (Not sure what the recommendations will be for COVID-19 going forward.) At or after age nineteen, you should have one tetanus-diphtheria and acellular pertussis (Tdap) vaccine as one of your tetanus-diphtheria vaccines if you did not receive it as an adolescent. You should have a tetanus-diphtheria booster every ten years. You should receive two doses of varicella vaccine if you never had chickenpox or the varicella vaccine. You should receive one to two doses of the measles, mumps, and rubella (MMR) vaccine if you are not already immune to MMR. Your doctor can tell you if you are immune.

Ask your provider about the human papilloma virus (HPV) vaccine if you are ages nineteen to twenty-six and you have (1) not received the HPV vaccine in the past, or (2) not completed the full vaccine series (you should catch up on this shot).

You can get a shingles vaccine at or after age fifty. I jumped on this. My mom had shingles and it is terrible.

Ask your doctor if you should get a vaccine to reduce your risk of pneumonia.

Infectious disease screening: Women who are sexually active should be screened for chlamydia and gonorrhea up until age twenty-five. Women twenty-five years and older should be screened if at high risk. All adults age eighteen to seventy-nine should get a onetime test for hepatitis C. Depending on your lifestyle and medical history, you may also need to be screened for infections such as syphilis and HIV, as well as other infections.

Breast cancer screening: A screening mammogram is not recommended for most women under age forty unless they have other risk factors. From forty to forty-nine, women may have a mammogram every one to two years. However, not all experts agree on this. Ask your doctor. Women fifty to seventy-five should have a mammogram every one to two years, depending on their risk factors.

If you are age eighteen to thirty-nine, your provider may do a clinical breast exam. (My gynecologist does one when I have my annual appointment.) If you have a mother or sister who had breast cancer at a young age, consider yearly mammograms. They should begin earlier than the age at which your youngest family member was diagnosed.

Cervical cancer screening: Cervical cancer screening should start at age twenty-one. After the first negative test, women ages twenty-one through twenty-nine should have a Pap test every three years. HPV testing is not recommended for this age group. Women ages thirty through sixty-five should be screened with either a Pap test every three years or the HPV test every five years. If you or your sexual partner has other new partners, you should have a Pap test every three years.

Women who have been treated for precancer (cervical dysplasia) should continue to have Pap tests for twenty years after treatment or until age sixty-five, whichever is longer.

Skin cancer exam: Your provider may check your skin for signs of skin cancer, especially if you're at high risk. People at high risk include those who have had skin cancer before, have close relatives with skin cancer, or have a weakened immune system. If you notice any spots or raised areas that change, ask your doctor to take a look. You know your body better than anyone. Twice my dermatologist thought places were okay, but when I insisted they had increased in size and she biopsied them, they turned out to be precancerous. Always ask.

Colon cancer screening: Talk with your provider about colon cancer screening if you have a strong family history of colon cancer or polyps, or if you have had inflammatory bowel disease or polyps yourself. Once you hit fifty, you need to be screened for colon cancer. Ask your doctor which test they recommend.

Other screenings: Lung cancer screening only if you are over age fifty-five and have been or are a smoker. Check with your doctor.

All women over age fifty with fractures should have a bone density test.

It is much easier to treat problems if they are caught early. Make those appointments.

- 15 -

SLEEP

Experts recommend seven to nine hours of sleep a night. Pay attention to your body. If you regularly get less than six hours of sleep a night, you are at higher risk for all kinds of health problems including diabetes, heart disease, stroke, cognitive decline, and death from any cause. A lack of restful sleep also makes it more likely you'll gain weight and have higher levels of stress hormones.

If that's not enough to convince you of the importance of sleep, your brain cleans itself when you're sleeping (I kid you not). Cerebrospinal fluid flows through the brain more freely when you're asleep and removes a harmful protein known as beta-amyloid that can build up and cause Alzheimer's disease. There is no excuse not to do everything possible to get a good night's sleep.

In addition, sleep is crucial for your performance. I can tell a difference in the quality of my speech if I didn't get enough sleep the night before.

Ever driven a car when you're exhausted? Nodding off at the wheel? You might as well be drunk! Pink Preppers need to be sharp to handle what life might throw at them. Sleep is an important part of your prep.

Here are some tips to improve your sleep:

- **Dark room, no screens:** The darker you can make your room, the better. I like blackout curtains. I travel with a sleep mask as well as chip clips to hold the curtains shut in hotel rooms. And step away from the electronics. They emit a blue light that's like a lightning bolt of alertness to your brain. I used to sleep with my Fitbit on because I wanted to track my sleep. Since it was attached to me, it was easy to check the time if I woke up in the night. Zap! A jolt to my brain, making it harder for me to go back to sleep. I quit wearing it to bed and sleep much better. Also, don't check your phone if you wake up in the night—zap! There is a blue-light-suppression feature in iPads and iPhones called NightShift you can access under Settings>Display & Brightness. But unless you are on emergency call, leave your electronics alone and get some sleep.
- **Quiet, cool:** We sleep with our dogs in the bedroom, and they make noise, not a ton, but it's there. This will mess with your sleep. If you're having trouble getting a good night's sleep, pets must go. When I travel, I take ear plugs. I have a white noise app on my phone in case I get desperate. Pink Preppers always have a plan to protect their sleep—it's that important. And the bedroom has to be cool. I've read different numbers for optimal sleep temperature from 60 to 68 degrees Fahrenheit. See what works for you.

- **Cut off caffeine, alcohol:** If I drink a lot of caffeine, I might be able to go to sleep, but then I wake up in the night. It disturbs my sleep. Try cutting caffeine off after 2:00 p.m. (or earlier) for a few days and see if you sleep better. I know I do. Many people have an alcoholic drink to help them go to sleep, but alcohol impacts the quality of your sleep and can have you awake in the middle of the night.

- **Keep a notepad by your bed:** Sometimes I start thinking about something and keep myself awake. To solve that problem, I keep a notepad and pen beside the bed and make a note to remind myself to deal with it in the morning. This helps me drop it and go back to sleep. I can't do anything about whatever awakened me in the middle of the night anyway.

- **Napping:** When desperate, I love a power nap. I've had some as short as twenty minutes and woke completely refreshed. The key is they can't be too long (for me—anything over ninety minutes and I can't sleep that night). You do you. Some people tell me any nap at all messes up their sleep that evening. Some people can't nap for more than an hour. Keep the power nap in your sleep arsenal. I get crabby if I'm exhausted. I also can't risk driving if I'm drowsy. Try a twenty-minute power nap if you have to get behind the wheel when you're tired—the life you save might be your own.

- **Exercise:** I sleep much better when I exercise. If you're having trouble sleeping and don't exercise, this is the first solution I would suggest. Add just fifteen minutes of physical activity during the day to start. You need to be exercising anyway.

- **Don't look at the clock:** We've all done it. You know how it is. You've got something important the next day or you have to get up outrageously early. You wake in the night and immediately look at the clock. "Oh no, it's only four! I have to get up in an hour. There's no way I can go back to sleep!" You're so alert and upset now, you can't go back to sleep. In this case ignorance really is bliss. If you didn't know what time it was, you might have been able to doze off for another hour. It doesn't matter what time it is; it matters that you get some sleep. Lay your pretty pink head down, don't look at the time, and go back to sleep. The alarm will tell you all you need to know.

- **Don't give up:** Many experts say if you can't sleep, don't keep lying there; after fifteen minutes or so, get up. I say bah. I lie there, work on clearing my mind and relaxing and, sooner or later, I go to sleep. If I were to get up at 2:00 a.m. and roam around the house, I'd be toast. I'd never get to sleep and would be a hot mess for the rest of the day.

- **Sleeping pills:** I'm not a fan. I'd say this should be a last resort. Pills have side effects, and you may find you are groggy the next day or have trouble waking up. They can also be psychologically addicting. Before you go this route, try everything else on the list and then do your homework. There have been a few times I was prescribed medication for minor issues, and when I read all the short- and long-term possible side effects, I decided not to take it. At the end of the day, the only person who has your back is you. Be responsible and read all the info before you take any medication.

NUTRITION

The science of nutrition changes all the time. It wasn't that long ago red wine was touted as a health elixir. You also have always heard that breakfast is the most important meal of the day. Well, turns out, not necessarily. (I've never eaten breakfast and have taken hell for that over the years, so I feel vindicated.) If you like to start your day with breakfast, do it.

Recommendations will probably change in a few years anyway. First the egg was bad, now the egg is good. What to do? Read. All Pink Preppers should read. You don't have to read a lot, but you should keep up with developments that could impact your health. (Reputable sources are everything, Pink Prepper. There's a ton of misinformation out there and social media is the worst.) Here are some I recommend:

- *Harvard Women's Health Watch*
- *Harvard Health Letter*
- *Tufts University Health & Nutrition Letter*
- *University of California, Berkeley Wellness Letter*

For specific concerns or questions, I look to the Mayo Clinic's website. Random Google searches can have you believing you have some exotic yet fatal disease. Snopes.com is an excellent fact-checking source if you hear some "medical breakthrough" that sounds too good to be true. Do your own research and then go see a pro.

Supplements: For years doctors would recommend taking a multivitamin (and many still do). The problem with this is twofold: (1) your body doesn't absorb vitamins from supplements well, and (2) you may be getting more of some vitamins and/or minerals than you need, which could have harmful effects.

Not long ago a doctor told me to take vitamin D. When I told him I was often in the sun, he scoffed. Well, Dr. Smarty Pants, it's beneficial to get some sun exposure—your body absorbs vitamin D best that way. Calcium and vitamin D supplement use is controversial. And did he even ask about my diet or what supplements I might already be taking? No.

According to Bess Dawson-Hughes, MD, director of the Bone Metabolism Team at the Human Nutrition Research Center on Aging, the best way to get calcium is through food. And vitamin D? The sun. Some people do need vitamin D supplements—those who don't get sun exposure, have very dark skin, or are obese.

I don't believe I know more than doctors. I do, however, think some doctors don't ask enough questions or listen to their patients. They prescribe vitamins because it gives them something to offer. But study after study shows the human body absorbs nutrients better from food than from supplements. My guess is doctors don't want to take the time to ask people about their diets, so they tell them to take vitamins.

You can keep spending that money and taking vitamins, but realize most of the vitamins are going in one end and straight out the other. In the case of calcium and vitamin D, rather than taking supplements, eat calcium-rich foods such as poppy seeds, cheese, and yogurt; increase bone strength through exercise; and get fifteen minutes or so in the sun every day. But again, if your doctor tells you otherwise, do what the doctor says. They know more about your health and your situation than I do. I won't go see the doctor I mentioned above again. My other doctors listen to me. Find one who listens to you as well.

Pink Prep Principle: Research any dietary supplement before taking it.

Superfoods: Here's the way to get your vitamins. I've created a list, but other foods could be added. Again, do your research and pay attention to your body. If you don't like any of these, find foods you do like. I love Nutella (who doesn't?), yet plain hazelnuts are too bitter for me. But there are a lot of other nuts I love. (Nutella has too much sugar to be a nutritional recommendation, but all foods in moderation.)

Why are these called superfoods? Because they offer a lot of bang for the nutritional buck. Some of them are the best way to get a vitamin (example: almonds and vitamin E), and they offer more than one benefit. Almonds also have iron and zinc and calcium.

- Berries
- Fish
- Leafy greens, tomatoes, broccoli

- Legumes (beans, peas, peanuts)
- Nuts
- Yogurt (low-fat Greek is best)

Visit your local grocer and farmers' markets and buy fresh, but there are loads of frozen and canned options as well. And, no, canned foods do not lose all their nutrients. Keep an eye on added sugar or salt. Canned fruit with no added sugar is delish and lasts forever. I found a blend of frozen blueberries, cherries, and strawberries at Target that has changed my life. I love the idea of eating the rainbow—but we're not talking Skittles, we're talking colorful fruits and veggies.

Some of you are already healthy eaters and have my undying admiration. I consider myself a semihealthy eater. I love sweets and I am not giving them up. But I don't eat red meat, fried food (except for once a year at the state fair—fried Oreos and Reese's are my BFFs), or tons of chips. My standard lunch is low-fat Greek yogurt, blueberries and nuts, or Fiber One cereal. Make this easy. Simply eat more superfoods (fruits, veggies, nuts) and less junk. You'll be surprised how delicious some of the healthy options available now are. Try them.

In the bonus section of this book is a tool you can use to fine-tune your diet. Along the top of one chart I've listed vitamins and minerals we might have a deficiency in (these numbers vary based on gender and age, but this is a general guide for women). You can fill in a day or two of your normal food choices and see how you're doing. After doing this, I decided to add Fiber One bran cereal to my diet. I was surprised at how little fiber I was getting, and Fiber One has iron and magnesium (since I don't eat much red meat, I need more iron). Vitamins from food are best. Taking too much iron in supplement form can cause problems.

Don't stress over this. Use the guide to determine if you could make a trade-off to incorporate something healthier in your diet. You may also discover you have some misconceptions about certain foods. I always thought dates = fiber. Well, calorie-wise, dates have as much fiber as fruit cocktail. Lots of packaged foods are labeled as healthy and are not necessarily so. This guide can help you see things more clearly.

Diets: People often underreport their weight, so obesity stats are hard to gather. But a study in the *New England Journal of Medicine* projected that by 2030 nearly 50 percent of Americans will be obese. Nearly one in four will have severe obesity. The CDC cites a myriad of health issues that come with obesity including heart disease, high blood pressure, type 2 diabetes, stroke, gallbladder disease, and increased risk of death from all causes.

Need I say more, Pink Prepper? If you are going to be serious about being ready for the worst, you have to work on being healthy. Obesity is not healthy. I'm not saying you have to be a stick-thin runway model. I've had cellulite on my thighs ever since I can remember. Most of us are far from those images of perfection we are inundated with (even the large models have no cellulite). But I don't care about that ridiculousness. I care about you being ready to handle what life will throw at you. I care about you being healthy.

In her amazing book, *The Unthinkable: Who Survives When Disaster Strikes—and Why*, author Amanda Ripley says, "The harsh truth is that obese people move more slowly, are more vulnerable to secondary injuries such as heart attacks, and have a harder time physically recovering from any injuries they do sustain." She goes on to remind us that "on 9/11, people with low physical ability were three times as likely to be hurt while evacuating the towers." One man was so obese his coworkers had to carry him down thirty-plus flights of stairs. Think of all the people trying to escape who were slowed by that one person. Losing weight can help the obese survive and help ensure they are not a burden to others.

So what is considered obese and severely obese (also called morbidly obese)?

The CDC website has information for assessing your weight as well as an online calculator. Enter your numbers and see where you are. As an example, the average woman in the US is 5 feet 4 and weighs 170 pounds, when 108 to 145 is considered a healthy weight for her height. The average American woman is obese at 170. And at 180 and up, she is severely obese. The average American woman is not prepared.

I know, I know, losing weight is not easy. I love to eat. I consider the Pillsbury Doughboy and Little Debbie close personal friends. But if you're overweight and don't stop the weight-gain train now, it will only get harder as you age. Your health will deteriorate more. If you are fit and do not have a weight problem (yes, the rest of us are jealous as hell), you can skip this section. The rest of us have some work to do.

Tips for Weight Management

In general, diets don't work. We all believe we'll go on a diet, lose weight, and then we'll go back to our evil ways. Yep, and we'll gain back all the weight we lost and probably more. So stop thinking about a diet. This is about changing your choices and habits and being healthier. Not for a short time. Forever.

You do you is more important than ever. I had a personal trainer develop an eating plan for me. It was full of chicken breasts and kale. There was not one thing on the whole suggested menu I liked. I thought, "If this is my future, I'd rather die now." Diets that work for some people don't work for other people. If you put me on a diet that allows the eating of unlimited quantities of cheese, I will approach the size of a small barn. I do better with eating large quantities of foods like fruit and salads and popcorn.

I mentioned earlier breakfast is not necessarily the most important meal of the day. I've never been a breakfast eater. I'm not hungry in the morning and if I do eat something, it makes me hungrier throughout the day. If you're trying to lose weight, you might investigate skipping breakfast and see what happens.

However, if you are healthy and love eating breakfast, you do you. I use this example because it's such a commonly held belief and turns out it's not necessarily accurate. If you're doing manual labor all day, then, yes, you need a hearty breakfast. We desk sitters don't need a lot of calories to check email. Do your homework, try different approaches, and see what works for you. However, if doing you isn't working, you gotta do something else.

All things in moderation or total abstinence. My dad is in the total abstinence camp. He had a weight problem when I was a kid. He ruined my childhood because we couldn't have any sweets in the house. I had a Pop-Tart at a friend's house and almost passed out from the sheer joy of it. I also realized how horrible my parents were to deny me this ecstasy. My dad decided sugar, bread, and all items made thereof would never pass his lips again and thus it was. To this day, he eats like Gandhi. He's in his eighties, sharp as a tack, and will probably outlive us all. I'm waiting for him to ascend to the mountaintop, he's so pure.

I'm in the "all things in moderation" camp. I say the hell with the mountaintop, hand me a Reese's Egg. But when my jeans get tight, I rein it in. What's healthier? My pop, definitely. Who's having more fun? Well, sorry, Pop. S'mores are way more fun than kale. However, I can't eat like that all the time. I have enough to keep me happy and keep me healthy. Whatever path works for you is the path to take.

Get knowledge—one of a Pink Prepper's most important tools. My friend Judy decided she wanted to go on a diet. She suggested we go to a restaurant with a salad bar. We both grabbed a plate. She proceeded to add lettuce, at least a cup of blue cheese dressing, tons of shredded cheese, scoops of bacon, and loads of croutons. I said, "Girlfriend, you might as well have ordered a burger and fries." In her mind, salad = weight loss. If you don't understand calories and how many some foods contain, you can't make better choices.

Calories really do matter. I hear you thinking, "Wait, you said diets don't work." I'm not saying you must go on a diet. I'm saying if you are overweight, you have to eat less for the rest of your life. Yep, read that again—you have to eat less for the rest of your life. There is no "diet." Let's begin by figuring out how much you can eat. One of my favorite tools is the National Institute of Diabetes and Digestive and Kidney Diseases Body Weight Planner: www.niddk.nih.gov/bwp.

You can mess with this and see how many calories are required each day to maintain or lose weight. You enter in your activity level and other variables and get a result. I can eat about 2,200 calories a day if I want to maintain my weight. If I want to lose weight, I need to eat less or exercise more.

Why do you need to know this? You are not going on a diet. You need to know it to make better choices for the rest of your life. How? Let's say we go to Cheesecake Factory for lunch. I'll get the Margherita flatbread, eat no bread, and have no dessert. Let's say you get the Barbeque Ranch Chicken salad and have one small piece of bread to go with it. My calories are 760 and yours are 1,400. If we split a piece of cheesecake? Add another 600 calories each. If you also drank a sweetened beverage, it's possible you've had all your calories for the day to maintain your weight. I don't tell you this to upset you; I tell you this to empower you. You can make better choices.

For example, I refuse to drink any added calories. Ever. I love to eat too much to drink my calories. That's an easy choice for me. You might start saying, "Lord, do not leave those Olive Garden breadsticks on the table. They are my kryptonite." (I don't know about you, but I can eat at least three and not even feel full—that's 420 calories. I could have had cheesecake.)

All I want you to do is make better choices. You don't have to starve. You can have a whole serving of Olive Garden's minestrone soup for 110 calories—less than a breadstick, way more filling and better for you. Am I saying never eat another OG breadstick again? My dad is saying, yes—never eat that devil bread again. I'm saying have one and two bowls of soup. You'll be healthier and fuller.

Are you with me, Pink Prepper? Learn, then choose better. Craft a way to eat that works for you. You'll be surprised at what might start to happen. Knowledge is power.

Know what derails you and plan accordingly. I am derailed by open grazing (buffets), chips and salsa, eating out of the bag, social events, and not being busy at night. Take a minute and make your list. If you don't already know what causes you to overeat, pay attention next time you feel like you ate too much. Then you can create a plan.

I am far, far, far from perfect, Pink Prepper. I love food. I screw up. But I keep my weight in the healthy range (and yes, there was a time when it was higher than the healthy range and I was overweight, so don't

say I don't understand you). I'm sharing my tips with you to help you be
healthy. To prevent derailments, I do this:

- Choose what I'm going to eat before I go to a restaurant. I
  check out the menu online. Most restaurants have nutrition
  info online and more and more are adding it to their menus.
  But if I wait to choose until I get to the restaurant, I'm much
  more likely to make a bad choice. This way I plan my meal.
  I might want to have a dessert, so I can eat something super
  light and still indulge. If I have no plan and go with the flow,
  I'll overdo it, eating breadsticks and dessert and everything
  in between. Planning ahead helps me save myself.
- I do not take the whole package, bag, box, whatever and
  snack out of it. If I do, I'm going down, baby. Before I know
  it, I'm thinking, "How did I eat that entire family-size bag
  of Cheetos?" I get a serving and step away from the pantry.
- I try to avoid buffets, chips, and bread baskets as much as
  possible. They all speak to me. They whisper, "Just have one.
  Everyone else is. You'll stop after a few." And "Just have
  a taste. Of everything." Or "You'll do better tomorrow." I
  find I've started many, many diets tomorrow. Some foods
  and situations I can't do in moderation and I have to move
  toward Dad's abstinence approach.
- After dinner is when I'm most likely to overeat. So I find
  something else to occupy my thoughts. I do laundry, catch
  up on email, read a magazine, clean out a drawer—anything
  to keep my hands and thoughts occupied. Boredom is a
  lousy reason to eat.

Eat more good stuff and less bad stuff. Swap some healthy things for some bad things. Fruits and vegetables = good. Chips, sweets, red meat, fried foods = bad. Try swapping yogurt and fruit for sweets. Hate yogurt? Try low-fat ice cream. Try a caramel rice cake with Nutella and strawberries instead of a bag of Oreos. Try to start making better choices, not lose thirty pounds. Baby steps add up.

Fix your relationship with your scale. Do not avoid the scale or obsess over it. It's only a measurement tool. Some people weigh every day and if that works for you, go for it. It makes me too crazy and frustrated because it doesn't always reflect my actions. I think, "I ate hardly anything yesterday and I gained weight? What's the point? Hello, swiss cake rolls!"

So I weigh every couple of days. If I wait too long, I can get too far out of my zone of acceptability. And the farther out I get, the harder it is to get back in. Ignorance here can make for a tough journey back. But don't stress and obsess. Your period, salty food, hormones—all can impact your weight.

Pink Prepper health hacks:

- **Snack-sized bags for portion control.** Costco carries some delicious trail mixes and nuts. Both of which can be healthy (check the labels) but also have tons of calories. My recent fav was 210 calories for a measly one quarter of a cup. Pink Prepper, I can eat a cup before I realize I've started (a whopping 840 calories). Don't try guessing or eyeballing. Those are emergency tactics only to be used in situations where measuring is a social embarrassment. I know I have no control, but I also know nuts are packed with nutrients. What to do? As soon as I open the container, I portion the contents out into quarter-cup snack bags. When I grab one as a snack, I know exactly what I'm doing. Remember, my pretty, you lie best when you lie to yourself. And I am really good at lying to myself about the size of a serving and my ability to not eat the entire container of almost anything. (I also suggest you fill these snack bags when you are not hungry.)

- **Find healthy foods you like and eat them all the time.** Every day I have the same lunch. I'm not grazing (disaster) or deciding what to eat when I'm hungry. I like it and don't have to think about it. When I'm home, I have a healthy lunch.

- **Plan your meals when you travel.** When traveling, I either take food with me or know where I'm going to eat. Room service has derailed me too many times. I believe I'm ordering something healthy and it shows up with a side of bread. If bread comes, I usually wind up eating it. Or maybe they didn't put the dressing on the side and drenched the salad. If I'm on a vacation, I enjoy my meals, but I travel too much to eat rich, high-calorie food all the time. Taking my own food also saves me if flights are delayed and everything is closed by the time I finally arrive.

- **Don't forbid anything.** If you want a fried Reese's Cup, you should have one. But all in moderation. If you can't handle having a certain food in your house, only buy one serving and savor it. When I tell myself I will never eat sweets again, they are all I think about.

- **Have a weight range you can live with (in the healthy weight zone).** This is the above-mentioned zone of accepta-bility. I feel many of us have a dream weight—that weight that we got down to once or twice and we looked amazing.

But it was impossible to maintain. Then we have a weight range where we feel good, look good, and can actually live life. Let's say you are of average height, 5 feet 4, and weigh 150. Your healthy weight zone is 110 to 140. Maybe you worked super hard and got down to 125, but it is way too hard to maintain. But you can maintain 130. Weigh yourself once a week and when you get over 135—you cut back. You let go of 125 (nice, but too dang hard to maintain), and you keep your weight in the healthy range. It's easier to lose five pounds than twenty pounds. Your zone of acceptability is 130 to 135.

- **Find a veggie side you like and have it all the time.** I love edamame. I keep frozen bags on hand, zap them in the microwave, add pepper, and eat up. They are a nutritional powerhouse, and I get them in their pods so it takes me longer to eat them. You simply can't go wrong by adding a veggie.

- **Have some healthy foods you can grab to stop a craving before you make a disastrous choice.** Low-fat string cheese is high in calcium and low in calories: 50 calories for 15 percent of your daily calcium and 6 grams of protein. And it's fun to eat! Fiber One's Cake Bars have only 70 calories and 5 grams of fiber. When you need something sweet, these aren't too bad. Fruit is better, but some days you just want cake. Find items that work for you.

- **Enjoy fifteen minutes of sunshine every day.** You need that sun exposure to get your vitamin D. And you can use a break.

- 17 -

EXERCISE

There is no eating program, no medicine, no magic amount of sleep that will help you prepare for the worst like exercise. From the CDC's website:

Science shows that physical activity can reduce your risk of dying early from leading causes of death, like heart disease and some cancers. This is remarkable in two ways:

Only a few lifestyle choices have as large an impact on your health as physical activity. People who are physically active for about 150 minutes a week have a 33 percent lower risk of all-cause mortality than those who are physically inactive.

You don't have to do high amounts of activity or vigorous intensity activity to reduce your risk of premature death. Benefits start to accumulate with any amount of moderate or vigorous intensity physical activity.

What? A 33 percent lower risk of dying from all causes! You must start exercising if you don't already. And walking, simply walking, counts. Not convinced? From the Mayo Clinic:

> Worried about heart disease? Hoping to prevent high blood pressure? No matter what your current weight is, being active boosts high-density lipoprotein (HDL) cholesterol, the "good" cholesterol, and it decreases unhealthy triglycerides. This one-two punch keeps your blood flowing smoothly, which decreases your risk of cardiovascular diseases.

Regular exercise helps prevent or manage many health problems and concerns, including:

- Stroke
- Metabolic syndrome
- High blood pressure
- Type 2 diabetes
- Depression
- Anxiety
- Many types of cancer
- Arthritis
- Falls

It can also help improve cognitive function and helps lower the risk of death from all causes.

Exercise helps your body and your mind, elevates your mood, helps you sleep better, increases your length and quality of life—this is a no-brainer. If you don't exercise, put this book down, and do ten jumping jacks. Feel your heart? It's cleaning out the junk in your arteries. That jumping also helps strengthen your bones. Time to get serious about your health. Start walking today. (If it's late, you can wait until tomorrow.)

If you already exercise regularly and are shouting, "Hell yeah!" you can skip this section. The rest of you need to listen up. I just gave you the silver bullet for living longer, being healthier, sleeping better, having more confidence, aging better, having less stress—the veritable fountain of health. And it's as easy as walking. Why in the world would you not do this? A measly twenty-minute walk each day would vastly improve your health if you're currently doing nothing. First, let's get rid of the excuses.

- **I don't have the time.** That's a joke—what you're really saying is, "I choose to do other things." You had time to binge watch Netflix. Is *Tiger King* more important to you than your health? I know it's not, so drop that lame excuse right now. You can darn well find twenty minutes. Please.
- **I can't do that much.** Maybe you have let your health go. You have severe knee pain or other issues. This is even more important for you than everyone else. If you can't walk for twenty minutes, can you walk for five? Start with what you can do and do it for thirty days. Then try to add a minute. No amount is too small, and anything is better than nothing. If you can't walk, can you swim? Ride a stationary bike? I know there is something you can do. The quality and length of your life is dependent upon you moving.

 I have two fake hips, so I'm not feeling sorry for you. I will cheer you on, I will give you the tools you need to be ready for the worst, I will celebrate your successes with you, but I will not pity you. Pink Preppers are powerful and no matter where they are in their journey, the fact that they are making it makes them strong. The moment you took a single step down this path you said, "I am powerful enough to be prepared." You can't control what life may throw at you, but you can absolutely control how prepared you are.

- **I don't have the money.** Money? What money? Walking costs nothing. You can get a used exercise bike on eBay for about $150. You don't have the money to live longer? Do you have the money for all the medical bills your poor health will generate? This is another lame excuse.

We all know the real deal—you don't want to. Well, my dear, Pink Prep is all about doing what you may not want to do today so you are ready for tomorrow. You exercise today so you can recover more quickly from the surgery you might have. You exercise today so you can survive the next pandemic. You exercise today so you can run around with your grandchildren. You exercise today so you'll have more tomorrows. So stop with the excuses.

Ideas to help you exercise:

- **Start small.** I love my Fitbit and if you can afford one, consider it. I was shocked at how few steps I took on some days. Start by wearing it and see how many steps you take on a normal day. Try to take 100 more steps each day for a week. If that's too much, drop it back. Make it simple. Walk in place for the first five minutes of a TV show. Walk around your office when you're on a phone call. The goal is to do something so small you have no excuse not to do it. Something is always better than nothing.

- **But keep increasing.** Once you've done the small thing for a month (or whatever time frame you will do it), increase it. Our goal is to get you to at least twenty minutes a day. If it takes two years, I'm okay with that. Just start and don't stop. I want you to reap all the benefits.

- **You do you.** If you like, have an exercise buddy. I love walking with my friends, it makes the time fly. Maybe if a friend can't go with you, talk with them on the phone while you walk. I love mysteries so I often listen to audiobooks while I walk. I can't wait to get out there to hear what's going to happen. If you like music, listen to that. Or podcasts. The key is to find something you enjoy. Join a meetup.com exercise group. I did a workout the other day on my VR headset. If you can find something you enjoy, you are much more likely to stick with it.

- **Pick the best time.** The best time is simply—when you will do it. I'm not a morning person, so there is no way I'm getting up to exercise. That plan is doomed before it even starts. If you are a morning person, try exercising first thing. You'll have increased energy for the rest of the day. If the only time you have available is your lunch hour, well, there you go. See what works best for you.

- **Let pain be your guide.** There are two kinds of pain for exercisers—one is the soreness that comes from working muscles differently or harder than they've been worked before. That's a good pain. Then there is the pain of injury. That is a bad pain. If you are new to exercise, take it easy at first. Muscle soreness is to be expected. Anything you are unsure about or that seems like an injury, stop and talk with a healthcare provider.

Lifelong exercisers will know the difference; their problem is more an unwillingness to stop exercising and give their bodies time to heal. (Over exercisers, you know who you are.) Overtraining is not a positive thing; you need to give your body time to rest and repair itself. I took a case of plantar fasciitis and turned it into a fractured heel by refusing to rest. Pain needs to be attended to or it will get worse. Even simple muscle soreness is a signal to take a day off or do a different exercise and let that muscle recover.

- **As with overeating, learn from what derails you.** You may find if you don't go straight to the gym after work, you won't get there. You may find if it rains, you don't exercise, so you need a rain plan. You may find if you wait too late to exercise, you're too hungry and don't have the energy to work out. You may find your exercise buddy is a slacker and when she doesn't show up, you don't exercise. If you learn from these mistakes, they aren't mistakes; they are lessons to strengthen your resolve. Next time, you will be prepared for them. Mistakes are lessons to make us more prepared in the future.

- **Every day is not necessary.** I used every day in my example because twenty minutes every day is the smallest amount to meet the recommended guidelines. I typically walk for seventy-five minutes five days a week. There often are two days when I'm stuck in meetings or on flights and can't do it. I also need time to rest and recover. I do stretch every day. The goal is at least 150 minutes of moderate exercise each week.

- **Add weights and stretching if you can.** I know you have a busy life and I'd rather you do something than nothing. If you have an active job, you may even get enough exercise during the workday. You could add a bit of weightlifting and stretching to maximize your health and fitness. But first, focus on getting that 150 minutes of moderate physical activity, and then you can add these. Ultimately, it's best to do it all, but I will take what I can get. Anything is so much better than nothing.

Do not feel overwhelmed. All you need to do is start tiny, baby exercise immediately. Get more sleep—try the tips to improve what you're already doing. Eat more fruits and veggies and less junk.

Ta-da! Small changes can have a big impact over time. Not much in life is more important than your health.

18

TRAVEL PREP

W omen are worried about crime and (unless experiencing domestic abuse) are most vulnerable when away from home. The Bureau of Justice Statistics, part of the US Department of Justice, issues a report titled *Criminal Victimization*. The most recent report (issued in 2019) indicates violent crime in the US is decreasing. (Globally, violence against women is, well, disturbing.) Overall statistics can be misleading, however, because the chance you will be a victim of a crime varies widely based on many factors:

- **Where you live or travel to:** Baltimore and Detroit are much more dangerous than Rapid City, South Dakota. People who live in cities have a higher chance of being victimized than people who live out in the country.

In her class, Understanding and Applying Self-Defense Strategies, instructor Tammy Yard-McCracken says there are four primary places where violence happens:

- Where young men hang out in groups (bars, sporting events, certain street corners)
- Where people go to consume alcohol or drugs
- Where boundaries are in question (gang territory, countries at war, some office environments)
- Where you don't know the rules (anyplace you are new to the group, location, or environment)

- **Whether there is drug and alcohol use:** Most offenders are under the influence when they commit their crimes. And being under the influence yourself can make you more vulnerable.
- **Whether you are with a group or alone:** If you are alone, your risk increases. Predators want you vulnerable.
- **Your appearance:** If you look weak or distracted, criminals want easy targets.
- **Who is in your life:** According to the Bureau of Justice Statistics, the majority of violent victimizations of women are committed by people known to them. Globally, the UN Women site states, "Some national studies show that up to 70 percent of women have experienced physical and/or sexual violence from an intimate partner in their lifetime." The tragic thing is the people most likely to hurt you are the people you know. It might not be a romantic partner; it might be that creepy coworker or neighbor.

I want to be 100 percent clear, crime is never the victim's fault—ever. It is always the perpetrator's fault. I just want you to be aware of what can increase the chances this might happen to you.

A Pink Prepper living in Baltimore who often walks home alone at night from work has a greater chance of being victimized than a Pink Prepper living in Cary, NC, who works out of her home. However, if you throw in a crazy ex for our Carolina girl, her chances skyrocket.

If you know what impacts the likelihood of being a victim, you can take steps to decrease your chances. I have listed in the bonus section several books on staying safe in a dangerous world. All written by experts (and all written by men). I mention all the books were written by men because they often have extensive sections on self-defense.

It is admirable to know how to defend yourself, but my focus is on doing everything possible to never get that close to anyone who would do you harm. I'm a middle-aged woman with two hip replacements, so while I plan to fight like a wildcat if attacked, I have no illusions about my ninja warrior skills. I plan to use my best self-defense weapon (my brain) to avoid all these creeps entirely.

That said, if you want to take a self-defense class, I encourage you to do so. If you have no choice but to live in a dangerous area or there are other variables that increase your risk, that could be an important prep for you. And some violence is completely random. The goal of Pink Prep is for you to do everything in your power to avoid dangerous situations and not be a target.

If you practice everything here (and don't stay with abusive partners), the likelihood of getting in a fight for your life is extremely low. You are much more likely to fall victim to a health issue. We overestimate the likelihood of random attacks because they are so scary, and the media make a big deal about them. Random acts of violence generate clicks. Heart disease, not so much.

However, don't ignore this section. There are some bad people out there. And while the chance of you being victimized might be low, the impact of violence is huge. If you have a daughter, she needs to read this. I encourage you to share this information with every woman you know.

Tips for Staying Safe

Walk in like you own the place. I was meeting a group of friends at a bar. I always hated to be the first one, sitting there alone, like a loser. As I walked in, my thoughts were, "I hate this, I wish they would get it together and show up on time." But I would be damned if I would show what a loser I felt like, so I tried to look cool and confident. Later, I was talking to a guy and he said, "Yeah, I saw you when you came in. You walked in like you owned the place." Fake it till you make it, baby.

Why is this important in staying safe? Because predators look for the weak. Several studies have been done to determine how evil people select their victims. Results indicate it has to do with the would-be victim's gait. What to do to avoid selection? Walk everywhere like you're on the runway. Hold your head high and walk like you own it, sister! Your stride isn't too long or too short, it's just right. Your arms swing. Your posture is straight—shoulders back, chin up. It is clear you have places to go and things to do. You are calm and collected—models on the runway never look nervous. You are not hesitant or distracted or exhausted or afraid. Runway models are not looking at their phones. You let your eyes slide over everyone. You see the predator and he's nothing to you. Looking down or away makes you look weak.

Consider the wild. Which animals do predators attack? The slow and weak. They don't want to mess with the strong, it's too much trouble. Human predators are the same. They aren't looking for the hot chick, they are looking for the weak chick. And they need to know that isn't you. Make life your runway from now on.

Do not look distracted or disorganized. Predators look for the distracted. If you are distracted, you might not see him approach. You might be more likely to do something stupid. Let's say you just got off a call and are juggling several shopping bags and digging for your keys. Joe Handsome offers to hold your bags "for a sec." You're caught off-guard, so you agree. You open your trunk; he shoves you in. True violence is hard and incredibly fast.

Pay attention as if your life depends on it. Every book written on the topic of personal safety talks about situational awareness. We all need to practice this every time we leave our homes, and most of us don't. In their book, *Left of Bang*, Patrick Van Horne and Jason Riley, say a human universal is that we are clueless. We bumble around and don't pay attention to what happens around us. Pink Preppers must be different.

Situational awareness as I define it means being hyperaware of your surroundings with your safety at the forefront of your mind. You pay attention to the environment and the people in it. Begin to practice this all the time.

You already practice it to some degree while you're driving. If you have ever noticed someone driving erratically and taken measures to avoid them, that's situational awareness. Or if you noticed children playing near the side of the road and slowed down in case they darted into your path, that's situational awareness. You are noticing something, predicting what could happen, and taking action to avoid something bad.

What to pay attention to? If you start paying attention, you get a sense of a place in normal circumstances. I live in the southern United States. If I walk into a convenience store, the cashiers are often bantering with the customers, there tends to be a buzz about the place. People are typically wandering the aisles, with an item or two in their hands.

If I walked into a store and it was completely silent, I would know something was wrong immediately. If I saw someone with the hood of their hoodie up, I would be concerned. (And the best course of action is to leave immediately.) Pay attention to the norm, so you'll know when something is going on.

Notice how many people are in a store or restaurant. Do a scan and notice if everyone looks appropriate. Hoodies over people's heads are not appropriate in most circumstances. A heavy coat in the summer is not appropriate. Someone looking around nervously is not appropriate.

Notice where the exits are. If something happens, you want to be able to get out.

If you are in a parking lot, always make sure no one is loitering. Notice if anyone is sitting in their car(s). If I park next to a woman sitting in her car texting, I probably won't care. If I pull up next to a sketchy looking guy, not texting and sitting in his car, it might be best to park elsewhere. Unfortunately, before I started practicing situational awareness, I probably wouldn't have noticed either of them.

If you are out walking or running, pay attention to vehicles. Do they slow? Turn around ahead of or behind you? The other night a car passed me while I was walking, and the driver said something to me. No big deal, I was in my neighborhood, maybe he was saying hi. I smiled, said hello and we both kept going. But for some reason (intuition?) I turned around and watched as he drove away. He slowed, turned into a side road and turned around. What the heck?

He stopped there for a while (I was a bit concerned and started walking faster). Then he headed back in my direction. I walked down a neighbor's driveway as if I were heading toward their house as the vehicle slowly passed. Now I was nervous and called Tim, asking him to come outside (I was almost home).

The car was idling near our house, between the house and me, facing in my direction. Tim came outside, and the car moved off, but the whole thing was weird. This was not a neighbor returning home to get a forgotten item. I don't know if I avoided a problem and I'm okay with not knowing. Always better safe than sorry.

Pay attention to anyone paying attention to you. Most people are in their own little worlds, doing their own little things. If someone starts checking you out, be careful. I'm not talking about that hot guy at the bar. I'm talking about that hot guy in the parking garage. There are places where interacting is expected and places where it's weird.

Size up the sketchy. So much of this depends on the situation. If I see someone sketchy and I'm in the subway in NYC with about 50,000 other people, I may disregard it unless he's near me. If I see someone sketchy, and I'm the only other person in a parking garage, I'm watching him like a hawk (or getting the hell out of there). If I see someone sketchy and I'm about to get on an elevator with him, I step back and wait for the next one.

Let's say you left the mall and are walking down the runway (yes, prepper, this is your world, and these predators are just in it). You see someone questionable. Here are some further details to notice:

- **Check out his hands.** Hands hold weapons. Be extra cautious if he is hiding his hands. You might also ask why is he not holding a cell phone? Most people look at their phones when they have to wait.
- **Determine if his presence makes sense.** Men are always waiting for their women to shop. But they usually do it in the mall on a bench. Or at the sports bar watching the game.

Or maybe sitting in their car with their phone. Unless this person is smoking, why is he here?

- **Notice his body language.** Fidgety? Nervous? Is he paying attention to you? Look for anything that doesn't seem right. Most people at the mall pay little attention to anyone else. Is he looking behind him? People seldom do this unless they are (1) up to no good and don't want to get caught, or (2) a Pink Prepper making sure some freak isn't following her.

- **Notice his clothing.** Does he have his hood up when it's hot outside? Unless it's cold, only bad guys hide their faces. Is he wearing a bulky jacket on a warm day? He might be trying to hide his identity or conceal weapons.

Practice the rule of three. If you notice three weird things, you'll need to act. But don't wait if your intuition alerts. If your gut says, "Get out!"—do so immediately. But let's say you're not sure. You see a guy in the mall looking around and acting nervous, but he's dressed normally. You keep walking. Maybe he's waiting on a date. On the way home you stop at a convenience store to get a soda. You follow a guy into the store who was looking all around before going in. You notice he has a jacket on and it's summer. His hand is in his jacket pocket where he might have a gun. That's three—get out. You didn't need that soda anyway.

But don't delay. One night I was running laps around the edges of a baseball field. It wasn't well lit or fenced in, but it was convenient, and I had run there many nights before. One of the corners had trees and was dark, but so what? There were houses nearby and I always felt completely safe. I made a couple laps and was heading toward the dark corner when I felt a jolt of terror.

To this day I have no idea why. I didn't see or hear anything—at least consciously. But I didn't hesitate. I didn't look for one thing, much less three. I immediately ran away as fast as I could. Did I avoid a terrible fate? Don't know, don't care. Fear is your friend—act.

Pay particular attention to transition areas. Transition areas are when you leave one environment for another. Leaving the safety of your car to enter a parking lot is a transition and you'll want to do a quick scan before you get out. Leaving the mall (or work) and going into the parking lot is another transition. Be aware and ready, not juggling packages and looking for keys. End a call or send a text before leaving the building. You need to do your runway walk to your vehicle.

Give yourself some space. When you make a tight turn, you might turn into trouble. If you have no idea what's around a corner, circle out wider than you normally would and stay alert. If you are driving, leave ample space between you and the car in front of you at stoplights. You don't want to get boxed in if something happens. Space gives you time to react—some ploys are designed to get you closer to the predator. Ted Bundy had a fake cast and would ask women for help loading his car. When they got close, he had them. Keep your distance.

Use your hands. You need to go someplace scary. Maybe you are traveling and the hotel you booked turns out to be in a bad area. After you park your car, you might want to activate Noonlight. Noonlight is an app you hold until you get to your destination. If you release the button and don't punch in a code, it alerts authorities to your position. Of course, they won't get there immediately.

Maybe you choose to travel with pepper spray or put your keys between your knuckles so you could use them as a weapon. Have a plan what you will do if you don't feel safe and must proceed.

Love the crossbody purse. Not only is it harder to steal, it keeps your hands free for doing whatever else you might need to be doing. Get one that zips or has a flap to keep unwanted hands out and to keep your stuff in. I had one with a hook closure and the contents spilled out when it fell over in the x-ray machine at the airport. Good grief.

The normalcy bias is your enemy. We expect tomorrow to be the same as today. We hear bangs and think, "Oh, that must be firecrackers." We believe because there's never been a shooter at the mall, there never will be. We think things like that don't happen here. If it's not the Fourth of July and you hear firecrackers, head in the other direction. Your normalcy bias is so strong you might open your door to a stranger, believing, "It's broad daylight and no one bad lives in our neighborhood." Dozens of women thought, "This guy looks nice. Nice-looking guys don't hurt women" before they became Ted Bundy's victims. Don't let normalcy bias blind you to danger.

Always trust your lizard brain (or your gut) or your woman's intuition. The lizard brain is the oldest part of your brain, the primal part that lives in survival mode. It sends you signals before your higher reasoning even knows what's happening. Women often ignore it because they want to be seen as nice. Do you wanna be nice and be robbed, raped, or murdered? Or are you okay with someone thinking you're a jerk if it keeps you safe?

One night in New Orleans, a girlfriend and I were walking down a side street and two men were walking toward us. Something didn't seem right, and I told her, "Turn around." She picked up on the urgency in my voice and we quickly turned around. Did we seem rude? Probably. Did I save us? I don't know, and I'm glad I don't. Pay attention and always trust your gut.

I stopped at a Cracker Barrel one evening to use the restroom. (What could be safer than a Cracker Barrel?) As I headed back to my car, I thought I heard someone call my name. I turned around and saw a man I didn't recognize approaching. He was between me and the restaurant. I can't tell you what it was, but my brain said, "Run!" I turned and bolted for my car. Did I escape or look like a freak? Again, don't know, don't care. Your intuition is faster than your reasoning and all it cares about is you. Listen to it.

If anyone ever approaches you, do not engage. You might only get hit up for money, but it might be worse. Sometimes women feel it is mean or rude to ignore or avoid someone in these situations. No, it is rude to make a woman on her own uncomfortable. Worrying about seeming rude will make you an easy target.

I'd go so far as to say every time a stranger has approached me, it's been bad. Seldom in the course of normal events does a complete stranger approach you. I'm not talking about a passing smile in the aisle of the supermarket or chatting with someone in line at Target. I'm talking about those incidents when, out of the blue, someone approaches you. It's usually because they are up to no good.

I'm a friendly person, but I'm also a suspicious person. When I'm out walking, if anyone stops their car to talk with me, I always stand well back from the vehicle. Always. One time a man stopped and initially he was fine, but I wouldn't approach. As I said goodbye and turned away, he made a nasty comment. I won't lie, it was scary. But I was far enough away that it didn't matter.

Pink Prep Principle: Never get near anyone's vehicle. If they are stopping, they want something.

The need to avoid these situations is an alien concept to most men. Ask yourself, "When was the last time I was afraid another person would harm me?" For most women it's recently. Now ask a man. He might give you a blank look. In *The Gift of Fear*, Gavin de Becker says, "At core, men are afraid women will laugh at them, while at core, women are afraid men will kill them."

Often predators are trying to get you to lower your guard. They might start by asking for directions: "Hey, how can I get to Green Street?" They may try to look innocent and polite, but your gut will warn you. Something will be out of sync.

Here's the truth—normal people do not want to make you uncomfortable. If a nice guy needed directions, he wouldn't approach a woman out by herself after dark. And with cell phones, does anyone need directions, the time, or anything else? What they want is to get physically closer to you and for you to let your guard down. Do not engage with random strangers who approach you.

Tim and I were in the Target parking lot and a man approached us offering to take our cart. As soon as he appeared, I went into "get away and get in the car mode." My sweetheart, however, thanked him and started chatting. He wound up giving the guy money just to escape. I was furious he even engaged.

I can look back and tell you now what my intuition immediately picked up on. The man was not walking into the store. Period—that is everything. If he were heading into the store, taking our cart might not be that big a deal. Unusual, but possible. However, that wasn't the case. He approached us from the store. He had no reason whatsoever to come and get our cart. (If anyone ever approaches you, do not engage. Many muggings begin with the words, "Excuse me.") He proceeded to engage in several pre-incident indicators (as identified in *The Gift of Fear* by Gavin de Becker):

- **Loan sharking:** Occurs when a predator offers help you never asked for, so you feel obligated to further engage with him, give him money. This guy offered to take our cart back. Another predator might offer to help you carry something or clean your windshield when you're stopped at a stoplight (an old NYC scam).

- **Charm and niceness:** This predator had a big smile and was overly nice and complimentary from the get-go. I was having none of it, but Tim was sucked in. And if you doubt the power of this, two words: Ted Bundy.

- **Forced teaming:** The predator implies you have something in common. Target cart man asked Tim if he was in the military and told him that he served. I was still trying to get the hell out of there. I was thinking, "Men, geez. Hello? Can't you see this guy is not going away?"

- **Discounting the word no:** Immediately, we said no thanks, we'd take our cart back. When he approached, we were still unloading it (giving him more access to us because we had to stay there). Normal people listen when you say no.

- **Too many details:** If someone is lying, they often add details to make them sound credible, more than you need or expect. This guy talked about his supposed military service and went into gross detail about his health problems. Clearly this had nothing to do with the cart. He launched into a detailed description of "war" injuries and finally guilted Tim into giving him money. This still makes me mad.

This predator never used the following techniques, but be on the lookout for them:

- **Typecasting:** The predator might label you in a way to make you feel you need to defend yourself. Maybe something like, "You rich girls don't have the time of day for hardworking guys like me." You find yourself protesting and, bam, you're in conversation with this nut job. Don't engage.
- **The unsolicited promise:** "One more drink and I promise I'll go home." "I promise we'll just cuddle." "I promise I won't hurt you." These promises are usually made to be broken.

We later learned this man had been asked to leave by Target management several times. The cart ploy had been working particularly well for him. What he does isn't robbery, but he gets people to give him money by making them feel uncomfortable in a parking lot. If I had been alone, I would have felt intimidated. But I wouldn't have engaged; my intuition immediately told me the situation was bad.

You may feel my use of the word *predator* here is too strong. But I consider anyone who invades my personal space, does not take no for an answer, and purposely makes me uncomfortable until I give him what he wants to be a predator. Are you worried about being nice again?

Learn from your experiences. Take a minute and remember all the times in your life your intuition kicked in. Consider the times you listened and the times you didn't. The challenge is, when we listen, we may never know if we were right (like my New Orleans and Cracker Barrel experiences). But if we don't listen, the consequences can be terrible.

Kelli and her husband were staying at a beach house when the owner told them workers would be coming by in the next day or two to install some cabinetry. The following day Kelli was sitting on the deck when a white van pulled up and two men got out. Immediately, she didn't like it. It bothered her so much, she went upstairs and got her husband's gun out of his bag. He, meanwhile, invited the guys in. She stayed upstairs and prepared to somehow save the day. Luckily, nothing happened, but they weren't the cabinet installers. They said they had the wrong house and left.

What tipped her off? The van had no company name or logo on it. It was solid white. When the men got out, they looked more like prison escapees than legit workmen. One had a shaved head and tattoos; both were wearing wife beater T-shirts, no uniforms of any kind. Did they do something bad at the other house? She has no idea. But she was right. They shouldn't have been at their place.

Usually I listen to my gut, but one time I didn't. A well-known speaker offered to give me business advice if I would come by his office. I thought he was creepy and wasn't planning to take him up on it. When I told some of my speaker friends about the offer, they said I was crazy not to go, that he could really help me. I respected them and thought, "Well, who am I to think he would want to hit on me, anyway?" So I agreed to meet at his office.

Turned out his office was in his home. No one else was there. He offered me a mint and gestured that he would pop it in my mouth (weird, but). When I opened my mouth for the mint, he leaned forward and stuck his tongue in my mouth (ugh—I'm still disgusted). He then said, "You know you want it."

Luckily, his cell phone rang, his daughter calling. He had to go and hustled me out of there, asking me not to tell anyone. He did say he would make my speaking career if I agreed to another "date." Date? My skin crawls as I write this. That was the only time I ignored my gut, and I am so thankful his daughter called when she did. Ignore your friends, ignore the idea that you have to be nice, respectful, or anything else. The only thing you have to do is trust your intuition.

There are more scams and scammers out there than you can imagine. I was sitting in a common area in an airport when a young man sat down nearby. My first thought was, "Why is he sitting so close to me when there are about a hundred other seats around?" Then he started a noticeably loud cell phone conversation saying, "They canceled my ticket, and I can't get home for the funeral. I don't have any cash on me, Grandma. I just need $20." Then he started to "cry." He looked over at me a few times before it clicked.

Ah! He was hoping I would offer him money. I got up and moved away but continued to watch him. As soon as I moved, his whole demeanor changed, and he ended his call. Didn't even tell "Grandma" goodbye before stalking off. If someone's behavior seems off or weird, pay attention and get away. Give your money to legitimate charities, not to strangers who approach you. Once you get out your purse, your vulnerability skyrockets.

Scammers can use props to lower your guard. Sandy was in the Amtrak station in Chicago looking for the stairs down to the platforms when a guy dressed in navy with a lanyard and an Amtrak hat seemed to materialize out of nowhere. He asked if she needed directions. She did. She had never been there before, and the area she was in was completely confusing. He gave her directions and then asked for money because he helped her. He tried to make her feel guilty by saying he lived off tips. She backed away quickly and said loudly, "Get away from me. You're a scammer." She walked away fast.

Predators are ruthless and will use whatever they can to get you to lower your guard. A lanyard and a blazer look official to most of us. We think someone on crutches is really incapacitated. We trust people in medical or law enforcement attire. Predators are wolves in sheep's clothing.

Situational awareness is not only about people. Standing on a street corner in Chicago, I was waiting for the crosswalk signal to change so I could cross. As soon as it did, I stepped forward. The next thing I knew, something smacked into my arm and spun me around. A bus ran the light and hit me. (Ever said, "What if I get hit by a bus?" Well, I did.) Thankfully, the woman next to me was a nurse and called an ambulance.

I don't know how, but my arm wasn't broken. I certainly wasn't practicing situational awareness. If I were, I would have looked to the left and seen a bus barreling toward me. That oversight could have cost me my life. Pay attention. (Needless to say, I no longer rush out when the signal changes.)

Tips for Improving Your Situational Awareness

People watch. I decided to start paying attention to everyone around me at the airport instead of reading. Three guys gathered near the luggage carousel. All were about the same age, but I couldn't figure out why they were there. One set a bag on the floor while they were talking. Their body language was completely normal. They chatted for a while; one picked up the bag and they moved on. I didn't foil any plots and, as far as I know, nothing happened, but I did practice my situational awareness.

Sit for options and visibility. In public places, sit where you can keep an eye on your surroundings. In the waiting room at the doctor's office, sit so you can watch the door. What if a crazy ex-husband comes in with a wild look in his eye? Wouldn't you like to be the one who slips out as he rushes reception? The sooner you see trouble coming, the sooner you can get away. At the airport, sit at the end of a row while waiting to board. It will be easier to leave if there's a fire or a bomb or a shooter. Always give yourself options in case you need to leave someplace in a hurry.

Have your spouse/friends/kids test you. Or better yet, test each other. You're on a family road trip and stop at a rest area. Your spouse might ask you, "How many people were in the car that pulled up next to ours?" You don't want to be the one who says, "What car?"

I pay much less attention when I'm with Tim and that's not wise. Sometimes I'm better at avoiding weirdos than he is. Men can be over-confident. They don't travel through the world as women do. Teach your kids to pay attention too. You can make it a game, asking, "The lady who passed us, what color was her dress?" This won't only help them stay safe, it will help them see other people, not just themselves and their electronics.

Have a plan for the worst. Ask yourself when you enter a new environment, "What would I do if there was trouble?" I'm wondering about my hair salon. If someone came in with a gun, I have no idea where the back exit is or if there even is one. If a fire broke out, I wouldn't know how to escape. I am clueless.

Do you know what most of us would do if there was trouble? Freeze. Yep. We would be like a deer in the headlights. If you don't have a plan of action, you will freeze. At a minimum, know where the exits are in any place you visit frequently.

Be hypervigilant in transitional spaces/situations. As mentioned earlier, you are particularly vulnerable in these spaces. Often you haven't had a chance to get your bearings and you're distracted. Other examples of transitional spaces are elevators, entries and exits, even public bathroom stalls. Pay extra attention when you are in these in-between spaces—you are more vulnerable.

Get out of the cell phone habit. Most people in public places are buried in their cell phones, completely distracted and noticing nothing. Spend the first few minutes in a new space simply sitting and watching. Resist the cell phone.

Look at your fellow travelers. If you regularly take the same train or bus or flight, pay attention to those traveling with you. If you recognize the regulars, you'll notice when someone stands out. I'm astonished at how many people focus only on their phones on public transport. You are trapped in a metal box with complete strangers. Looking at your phone is like closing your eyes.

Do you honestly believe you're that safe? Start taking a careful look around when you board (where are the exits, who is surrounding you), whenever there is a stop (and new people get on), and anytime your spidey sense tingles. Don't look at your phone until you feel safe. If SHTF, you need to be prepared to act. That text or email won't do a damn thing to help you.

Watch videos online. There's an excellent YouTube channel titled *Active Self Protection* with videos of real crimes and situations. This is not to upset you, it's so you can see what real violence looks like. It's nothing like in the movies. It's fast and terrifying.

There are also videos on the Department of Homeland Security's website that let you practice your awareness. They are part of the Department's If You See Something, Say Something campaign and can be found at https://www.dhs.gov/see-something-say-something/take-challenge.

They are lighthearted, but if we would all get off our cell phones and pay attention, the world would be a safer place. When did we decide that ignoring our fellow man was the best course of action?

Mix up your routine. It's easy to become complacent when you do the same things every day. It's also easier for predators to target you. Instead, try a different route to work or a different way home. Eat at a different restaurant or a different location in your office building. Go to different places on the weekends. Stay sharp.

Use all your senses. Some threats may have a smell. Walking one day, I noticed the air smelled different. There were some fires nearby—not a threat but they could have been. Also listen. We're all walking around with ear buds on. We could miss someone walking up behind us or far-off gunfire. Sometimes places are too quiet and that could be an important signal. Your senses were designed to keep you safe—use them.

General Safety Tips

Practice enforcing boundaries. Start by not saying yes when you want to say no. "No, thanks so much for the lovely invitation, but I don't want to go to your third baby shower." "No, I don't want to give up my exit row, window seat so you can sit next to your boyfriend." I saw a woman say no, and she immediately became my hero. She was totally nice, but it was a long flight and she wanted her extra exit row legroom. Good for her. You deserve the seat you paid for, and if you want to sit there, sit there. Since when do your needs come last?

Enforcing boundaries gets easier as you get older and more confident. The more you do it, the easier it gets. I'm not saying don't help people when you want to; I'm saying don't be the world's doormat. It makes you more likely to be someone's victim.

Set boundaries at work. If you are speaking and someone interrupts you, smile and say, "Excuse me. I wasn't finished." As someone who gets excited and interrupts others (I know, it's terrible, I'm working on it), if someone does this, I feel terrible for interrupting them. I also respect the hell out of them.

You deserve not to be interrupted. Instead of always agreeing to work late when everyone else leaves on time, simply smile and say, "I'm so sorry I have to get home tonight."

Practice this skill with those aggressive kiosk salespeople at the mall (the ones who come out and try to get you to put on their facial cream or look at cell phone covers). Ignore them and keep walking. They want you to engage with them. They'll try almost anything because they know if you engage, you may buy something. Ignore them and walk the runway. You're not being rude; it is rude for them to be so aggressive. The more you practice, the less likely you will be a victim.

Have some lines ready. If someone approaches you for cash, keep walking down the runway and say, "Sorry, I don't carry cash." Someone approaches you for directions, keep walking down the runway and say, "Sorry, I'm not from here." The cashier asks you to donate to a charity, "Sorry, I've already given." If you have a line ready, it is much easier to deliver it when you are put on the spot.

Alcohol makes you a target. Drunk women are easier to attack than sober women. They can make poor choices like deciding to stay at the bar despite their earlier agreement to leave with their friends or letting a man they just met drive them home. They may also be unable to defend themselves. Be extra responsible and careful when you drink.

All of this applies to drug use too. Drunk/high people are more vulnerable than sober people.

Boss your friends. Someone has to do it. During a high school trip to Paris, I was on the metro with friends who were giggling and acting like the stupid tourists we were. It was late at night, and I noticed we were being watched by the scattering of men on the train. I told them to hold it together. I've been the designated driver for years. I'm far from perfect, but I'll boss you if I believe it will help you. Now that you're a Pink Prepper, you carry the responsibility for spreading the word and protecting the other women in your life.

Don't be a flasher. Never flash cash and always be hypervigilant around ATMs. Criminals want something—and cash is king. They also want watches, jewelry, and electronics. Am I saying never wear nice jewelry? Nope. I'm saying if you have expensive items, there might be someone watching who wants them. If you are going to your favorite restaurant and will use valet parking, then rock that bling, sister! If you're going out dancing in the Village in NYC and will be walking several blocks, maybe leave your five-carat diamond at home. Tuck your purse under your coat or your necklace in your blouse. When you are in public, criminals may be watching you. And if you have something they want and feel it will be easy to take, they may try. Don't make yourself a target.

Stay with crowds in well-lit areas. You are more vulnerable if you are alone. If attending a conference, engage in activities with other attendees rather than go out on your own. Ask front desk people for advice before you venture off alone. At a conference in Atlantic City, the front desk woman suggested I not go solo to the waterfront at night. (I didn't.) Don't assume a man won't go in the women's restroom. Be careful any time you are isolated.

Never forget people's true relationship to you. Technology can give us a false sense of security. You may be on a dating site and have exchanged many emails and texts with someone. You may feel like you know him. You don't. He is a stranger. When meeting for the first time, always meet in a public place such as a crowded bar or restaurant. Pick a place you know and where you feel comfortable. Same thing for selling something on Craigslist. Don't let someone come to your home when you're alone. Meet in the Walmart parking lot during the day and where there are security cameras. All these people are strangers, and they do not get that kind of access to you.

What if you can't avoid a bad situation? Every situation is different. There are stories about women who talked their way out of an abduction and others who weren't so lucky. If something happens, always trust your intuition. Don't engage with anyone who approaches you randomly. If, despite all your best efforts, you find yourself in a bad situation, do this:

- **Give him the goods.** There are two types of predators: those who want something (your purse, your car, your laptop) and those who want to commit violence for the sake of violence. (Violence itself is the goal.) Give the first type what he wants, and he will probably go away. So give up the purse, keys, whatever. They are not worth dying for. Throw your keys or purse at him and run toward the exit, toward people, toward the light.
- **Don't insult him, challenge him, or threaten him.** Doing so could keep the predator from just leaving with the goods and instead deciding to shut you up.

- **Never go to a secondary location.** This is universally agreed upon. Drop to the ground, scream, kick, do whatever you can so you are not taken anywhere. The reason is twofold: (1) the chances of anyone finding you plummet, and (2) the odds are your abductor will kill you. Most rapes and murders are committed at a secondary location.

- **Move!** This depends on the threat, but the chances of a gunman hitting you if you are moving are low. You may feel you need to drop to the ground, or you might try to hide, but if you can run away, that's the thing to do. If you hear "firecrackers," head away from the sound to the nearest exit. Get away, get out. During 9/11 several people were calmly gathering their belongings rather than exiting the building. Don't let your normalcy bias numb you. Take action and get away.

Special Tips for Staying in Hotels

- **Check and make sure the doors to adjoining rooms and sliding doors or windows are locked.** You never know. (I often find balcony doors unlocked.)

- **Trust your gut.** I arrived at a hotel that was so sketchy, I left and drove all the way home instead of spending the night.

- **Always practice situational awareness.** Pay attention in the lobby. Better to delay heading to your room than have a weirdo follow you. Same with getting off the elevator. If someone is going to the same floor, you might get off on a different one so he can't follow you.

- **Choose the right room.** Aim for the third to sixth floors. The lower floors could be targeted by burglars because they can get in and out quickly. For the same reason, pass on rooms near stairwells. Above the sixth floor, firetruck ladders might not be able to reach you. Take the time to locate the fire exits before you go to sleep. Another reason for avoiding lower floors is noise. I had a video crew load their van by the window of my first floor room at 3:00 a.m. They were not quiet.

- **If the fire alarm goes off, get out.** I can't believe I have to write this, but I've lived it. I was in a hotel when around 2:00 a.m., the fire alarm went off. I grabbed my purse and immediately exited the building. From the parking lot, I could see people in their rooms looking out the windows. The next morning a woman told me she called the front desk to see if it was a drill. Another said she was waiting to see if someone would come and get her. Seriously? If the alarm goes off, get out.

Special Tips for Uber/Lyft/Car Rentals

- **Always match the license plate with the one on the app.** Make sure you get in the right car. Don't trust anyone who randomly offers you a ride—work through the app.
- **Ride in the backseat.** You'll have two doors to exit from and it gives the driver space. If they invite you to sit up front, smile and get in the back.
- **Share your route with someone.** I have Uber set to share my route with Tim. You might choose someone you're meeting later or your boss if you're on business.
- **Follow the route to make sure the driver isn't taking you to another location.** I often get new drivers and some of them don't even know their own cities. Do this if you take a cab as well.

- **If you're renting a car, take your time.** Adjust the mirrors, know where the lights and the windshield wipers are before you put it in drive. I was driving a rental car in Boston one night and it started raining. I was blinded and couldn't find the wiper switch for what seemed like hours. I'm lucky to be alive. (I've also flailed around trying to find interior lights, side mirror adjusters, turn signals, and headlights.) Find everything before you put the car in gear.

Want to carry mace or pepper spray or a taser or a gun? All that is up to you, but whatever you do, learn how to do it right. Don't carry a gun unless you are well trained and willing to kill someone. Also know what you can and can't carry on an airplane if flying.

Pink Prepper Protective Path: When away from home, pay attention. Stay in the light and around people. Walk the runway and don't be on your phone, especially in transitional spaces. Avoid people who approach you when it's not expected. Above all, trust your intuition.

19

AUTOMOTIVE ISSUES

While in your vehicle, you might have car trouble or be in an accident. You might encounter bad weather or unexpected detours or road raging drivers. It pays to prepare.

Pick a reliable vehicle. When you do buy a car, choose a dependable one. If you live in an area with a lot of snow and ice, rear-wheel drive is not your friend. Take care of whatever car you have. Change the oil according to what the owner's manual recommends (not what oil change rip-off places do). Newer cars don't require much maintenance, but you do need to change the oil. This seems ridiculous, but I knew a woman who simply never changed her oil. Her engine almost completely locked up. Change the oil. Take care of your vehicle—after all, you trust it with your life.

Always practice situational awareness. I am often driving alone at night. Sometimes I need to stop and use a restroom. Before committing to a place, I check it out. If I don't see multiple cars and a well-lit parking lot and interior, I'm not stopping. If I see anyone I consider even remotely sketchy hanging around outside, I drive on. If you see anything at all that gives you the slightest pause, drive on. If you aren't paying attention, you might blindly walk into a bad situation.

This means you look for gas before you need it or you won't have choices. I try to keep my gas above a quarter of a tank. Prepper rule—always fill up when you approach a quarter of a tank. If you're traveling at night or out in the boonies, begin to look for gas when you approach half a tank.

Parking lots can be dangerous. If it's dark or you are in an underground or deserted lot, as soon as you get in your car, lock the doors, put on your seat belt, and head out. If you're alone, this is the perfect opportunity for a predator to try to get in your car and attack. A light on in your car makes you highly visible to those outside. And makes them much less visible to you.

I didn't know this was a big deal; I've often sat in my car getting organized. I always felt safe once I got in. Once again, clueless human. At least get in the habit of locking the doors as soon as you get in.

Pick a safer spot. Often you'll have no choice. But at night, try to park in the light and close to the entrance. I always move fast when I have to park far away and it's dark. I look around and make sure no one questionable is nearby. If there is an obvious fellow traveler, I keep an eye on them. If the traveler is a female, I'll try to stay closer to her as we head toward the building—safety in numbers.

Keep the doors locked and the windows up as you drive. You don't want to be stuck at a stoplight and have some freak reach into your car. If you are driving along a highway out in the Nevada desert, woohoo—roll the windows down. But in populated areas, be aware. And if anyone you don't know approaches you, don't roll the window down for them. If they are normal and nice, they won't mind. In fact, they'll change their approach.

Many years ago (before GPS) I was driving on back roads at night and had gotten completely lost. I turned into a gas station. It was closed, but the lights were still on over the pumps. I pulled in, turned on my interior light, and started looking at a map (yep, old school).

Suddenly there was a knock on my window! A man was standing there motioning for me to roll down the window. My eyes were the size of saucers as I shook my head no. He realized I was afraid and took a big step back from the car. He asked if I was lost and proceeded to give me directions through the rolled-up window. (I cracked it half an inch to thank him.) Good people do not want to scare you, they want to help you. But just in case, keep your windows up.

Be careful when getting gas. There is something called sliding where a criminal "slides" into your car while you are preoccupied pumping gas or paying and takes your purse (or whatever valuables they can grab). You can see videos of this online. When you leave your car to pump gas, the criminal crouches down, opens the door on the other side of the vehicle from you, grabs your purse from the passenger seat, and takes off.

Get in the habit of either taking your purse with you when you pump gas or always locking the door. I didn't even know this was a thing. I've left my purse on the seat hundreds of times while pumping gas. Yep, clueless.

Keep wide open spaces. Leave plenty of space between you and the car in front of you. Do it when you stop, so if you had to get away, you could maneuver around. Do it when you drive in case the driver in front of you slams on their breaks. Most of us drive much too close to the car in front of us.

I'm also a big fan of the wave. If you do happen to do something stupid, cut someone off accidentally, pull out in front of someone you didn't see, always give them a wave. Deescalating rage is a good thing. Can't hurt, might help, and always makes you feel better.

Accidents

Always have your phone (and a car charger for it) with you and your emergency contact information both on the phone and printed/written out in your glove box. I have mine in a folder with my insurance info and my vehicle registration. Your phone might be lost in the crash and responders will check the glove box and your purse if you are incapacitated.

Always wear your seat belt. Period. Princess Diana might have lived to meet her grandchildren if she had been wearing a seatbelt. She died at the age of thirty-six.

As always, practice situational awareness. If you are in an accident late at night or in the middle of nowhere and you don't feel safe, don't get out of the car. Don't get out if the other driver seems super upset or weird in any way. Move your car to a safe location, lock the doors, and call the cops.

Car Trouble

I was driving home on a gray winter day. The night before it had been extremely cold. As I cruised along in my 370Z, a zippy little sports car with rear-wheel drive, it started to sleet. Because it had been so cold the night before, the road immediately was coated with ice. A tractor trailer jackknifed. When I tried to stop at a red light, my car slid right through the intersection. Cars were slipping and sliding everywhere.

I had to get off the road. I turned into a storage unit facility with a large parking lot. The lot was filling up quickly as more and more people realized how dangerous the roads were.

Little did we know when the storm started, all the schools across Raleigh let out. Everyone in the city was on the road, trying to leave work, get home, or get their children. Traffic was gridlocked by accidents and road conditions. People were running out of gas while stuck in traffic creating more lane closures. It was a disaster and Raleigh made national headlines for shutting down because of a half-inch of sleet. Everyone thought it was hilarious.

Well, it wasn't so funny sitting in that parking lot wondering how the hell I was going to get home. A woman came over and knocked on my window. She said she was a nurse and had to get to the hospital to work. She said, "Come with me. I'm going to stop someone with a truck and get into the city. I have to get to the hospital, and if both of us go, we'll be safe."

I thought this sounded like a damn fine plan. She was gutsy. (She was a nurse, after all.) We marched out through the snow (yes, now snow on top of the ice) to a man driving a white pickup for a utility company. At first, he pretended not to see us (who could blame him?). She knocked on the window, he opened it and listened to her plan. He looked a little alarmed at first, but said, "Okay, hop in. We're not going anywhere right away, but you're welcome to ride."

The three of us were in the truck for over four hours. He took her to the hospital and took me on to my house. By this point we had all exchanged contact information and were buddies. The next day it was much warmer, and it was easy to retrieve my car.

Was I Pink Prepped? Absolutely not. I did not have an extra pair of shoes (only the heels I was wearing). I was completely unprepared (no blanket, no food, no water) to spend the night in my car, and the last thing on my mind was asking some stranger for a ride. But that nurse jumped into action immediately. She knew there was safety in numbers. She picked a business vehicle that could get through the weather and moved so fast the driver didn't even have time to say no. What a rock star. (Every nurse is a Pink Prepper in my book.)

Did I learn from that experience? Start carrying items in my car I might need if I run into problems again? Nope, normalcy bias kicked right back in. Also, that was what is referred to as a near miss. Something quite bad could have happened, but it didn't. So I ignored it.

A word about the near miss. These happen all the time. Someone drives home drunk, doesn't get in an accident, so they consider it no big deal. You veer into another lane while texting, but it was empty, so you think nothing of it. You didn't lose your job in the COVID-19 pandemic, so you believe you're safe. We ignore near misses all the time. Pay more attention to them.

After the out-of-oil incident I mentioned earlier, I got a clue and put together a bag for my car with the items listed next. You don't have to get all these items. Instead, make a prioritized list of what you feel would be helpful to you and gather the items gradually. Then leave them in your vehicle.

Also, if you take something out, always put it back. Don't eat your protein bar one trip and not replenish it. It's too easy to do that and defeat the purpose. Adjust this list based on where you live and the reliability of your car. If you live in Florida, you probably don't need an ice scraper (in a pinch, use a credit card to scrape ice). If your car is older, you may need more repair items. (Most people don't need to carry oil with them, but if your car leaves oil stains in the driveway, add it to your list.)

What to Keep in Your Vehicle

I have all this is in a small duffel bag I leave in my car at all times.

Flashlight: I have one I can hold and one that hooks to the hood if I have to mess with the oil or fluids again. Also toss in some extra batteries. A large, heavy flashlight can double as a weapon.

Ice scraper and brush: You may need additional items if you live where there is severe winter weather. Consider a bag of cat litter or sand to give you traction when stuck and a small shovel. Or a moving van to relocate.

Fix-a-flat: I'll be honest, and this is so not Pink Prepper of me, I can't change a tire. And as long as there is fix-a-flat, I don't plan to. I've been lucky, I've had three flat tires in almost forty years of driving, and every time I was near a gas station or auto place where I could get help. Lucky. Not prepared. Shame on me.

Shoes you can walk in (not flip flops): Leave a pair of tennis shoes or hiking boots (again depending on where you live) in your vehicle. You don't want to be in a storage facility parking lot in an ice storm in high heels. Yes, my stupidity knows no bounds.

Umbrella and rain jacket: During my oil disaster I was trying to hold an umbrella, use my phone as a flashlight, and check the oil, all while keeping an eye on the unseemly guys in front of the convenience store. What an idiot. You might not be able to hold an umbrella and do what you need to do—carry a child, work on your vehicle—so toss in a rain jacket or pocket-sized poncho (a garbage bag is an option when you're out of options).

Bottle or two of water: There's something you should know called the survival rule of threes. You can survive three minutes without air, three hours without shelter in a harsh environment, three days without water, and three weeks without food. (How long you can survive without wine or chocolate is another matter.) Add a bottle or two of water. I also have a LifeStraw (www.LifeStraw.com) to purify drinking water. This way, if something completely outrageous happens, I can make it longer than three days (unless I'm in the desert, in which case it's pretty much curtains for me).

Heavier jacket or blanket: In North Carolina our weather overall is mild, but we can have cold temperatures in the winter. It doesn't hurt to have a survival blanket in the car. If you live in Florida, don't bother. You, tropical prepper, need sunscreen and bug repellent.

Jumper cables or, better yet, a car starter: I didn't even know these existed. They are little batteries that can travel with you and jump your car if needed. The beauty of these? You don't need another car to jumpstart yours. You don't have to ask the serial killer to pull over and help you: "Hi, my name is Ted." They are much more expensive than jumper cables and you have to keep them charged, but if you have a beater car, one of these starters might be worth its weight in gold to you.

Roadside service: I have AAA. I've never had to call them, so I personally can't vouch for them. But several of my friends can. At this writing a basic membership is affordable, and they will come and jump your car or fix your flat, get gas, open a locked door. I save enough in hotel discounts to pay for my membership. You can even use it if you're in someone else's car. This is a thoughtful gift for your daughter if she won't buy it for herself. However, you may already have roadside service with your auto insurance company or vehicle dealer, so make sure it's worth it for you.

Food that will last and not melt: Leaving a Snickers bar in a hot car is an act of treason in my book. It will liquify. You don't need your whole pantry, but you never know when a few granola bars might come in handy. Or a jar of peanut butter. Lots of calories and will last a long time. Just add a spoon to your bag.

Extra eyewear: I carry a contact lens case and an extra pair of glasses. Some of you won't need these, but there have been times when I regretted not having them. Backup sunglasses are vital. They are easy to lose and it's tough to drive in the blinding sun.

Handwipes or hand sanitizer: I need these to protect me from all the deadly germs everywhere, but more importantly for when I eat ice cream cones in the car. I stash handwipes everywhere. So useful. You may think, "I already do that." But if you didn't have tons when the pandemic hit, you're not doing it right. I keep these in the glove box, console, and the duffel.

Paper towels and a roll of toilet paper: Paper towels are useful for cleaning condensation or mud off windows or headlights and taillights and the backup camera. Also helpful if you have to clean off the dipstick or your hands. And you never know when some extra toilet paper could come in handy.

Cash: Someplace in your car, hide some cash. One day I was puttering around in my office and realized with a shock I should have left thirty minutes earlier for a speech. I was in a blind panic, grabbed my keys and my stuff and took off. I got about halfway there and realized I left my purse at home! No lipstick and, worse yet, no money. I arrived in the nick of time to take the stage (with no lipstick), apologizing profusely to my client. If that is not horrible enough, I had to borrow money from my client to put gas in my car to drive home. Talk about mortification.

Do not be me. You never know when having $20 in your car could make a huge difference. What if your credit cards get rejected and you need gas to get home? That's what prepping is all about—you never know. And as I write this, I realize I spent my last $20 from my car and I need to replenish right now. (That's how easy it is to forget.)

First aid stuff: I don't have much of a first aid kit. I figure if I need anything serious, I'm calling 911. It's probably better if I don't try to practice medicine. If you have children and skills, add one.

Backup meds: Speaking of medicine, if you or your children take medication on a regular basis, have extra in your vehicle bag. I carry Aleve and Tums.

A roll of duct tape: Maybe I'll duct tape my blanket over the windows so I can get some sleep or use it to seal a window crack. Maybe something will break and I'll duct tape it back together. I also have scissors, which I have actually used from time to time.

There are loads of other items I could add to this list—emergency cones and or flashers to set up if your car breaks down at night. If you often travel out in the wilderness, you might need tarps or paracord or multitools and fire starters. If you travel in areas with frequent snowstorms, you may need heavy boots, extra gloves, and a bear rifle. Most of us will just call AAA or 911 while we eat a granola bar and sip water. (The books in the bonus section can help Pink Preppers who spend time in the wild.)

If you think, "Well, I have that in my purse"—STOP. This is *in addition* to what's in your purse. You might forget it or have your purse stolen. Or use up what's in there. Toss some extra stuff in your vehicle. You can thank me later.

If you do get stranded in your vehicle, should you stay or should you go? That depends. In my winter storm example, I left my car and it turned out okay. If the amazing nurse hadn't approached me, I would have probably spent the night there. In most cases, you'll be able to call and get help, so sitting tight is best. But if your car slid way off the road, you don't have cell coverage, and you saw a McDonald's about a half mile back, you might head out.

Before deciding to leave your vehicle, consider the following:

- The car can provide shelter if the weather is bad.
- If it runs and has fuel, your car can keep you warm or cool.
- It makes you more visible to would-be rescuers.
- The car has other resources—power for your phone, light (to see and to signal), a horn to signal.
- Distances are farther than you realize, especially in bad conditions. If you haven't walked a mile in ten years, hiking back to the last exit may be much harder than you think.
- Don't leave until it's daylight and place a note on the dash-board with your contact info and plan. I didn't know to do this. If the nurse and I had been abducted, no one would have had a clue. If someone offers a ride, make sure they see you as you take a cell phone photo of your rescuer and the license plate and text to a friend.
- Do you even know where to go to find help? What if you get lost? If it's cold, you could die from hypothermia. If visibility is poor, you could get hit by another car. If alone, you might be picked up by a predator.

Hopefully, you will never be in a situation so dire you contemplate abandoning your car and walking to safety. If you have the recommended items in your car, you should be prepared for almost anything that could happen.

The Get Home Bag

Preppers have two bags: a Bug-Out Bag (I will discuss this in more detail later) and a Get Home Bag. A Bug-Out Bag is used when you have to leave home in a hurry. A Get Home Bag is used when you are away from home and have to get back.

When would you need such a thing? Maybe during a natural disaster or social unrest or a nuclear event. Think that's crazy? Last night I completed a survey from the nearby nuclear plant asking how quickly we could leave if an evacuation was ordered. I've been ordered to evacuate twice due to approaching hurricanes. This is definitely a thing.

Pink Preppers with the items recommended in their vehicle already have a Get Home Bag. If a Pink Prepper is stuck in her car for a night, she'll be okay. But this assumes we'll have access to our cars. If I'm out speaking and someone steals my car, well, there goes that plan. If that's the only thing that happens, I'll have my phone in my purse and I can call an Uber (after I call the cops, of course). But if I'm out speaking and there's a riot and my car is set on fire, I'll probably be in high heels and won't have anything.

Hard-core preppers put together a Get Home Bag and carry it everywhere. If you're in a situation where you don't have your car (maybe you carpool) or you use public transportation regularly, you might need to create a Get Home Bag and carry it with you (or keep it at your office).

Here are some items to consider in a Get Home Bag:

- **The bag itself:** Should be easy to carry. It needs to be large enough to contain what you might need if all hell broke loose (think 9/11) and you needed to get home (or at least to safety).
- **Shoes:** You might have to walk or run. You need the right shoes for this.
- **Cash:** I'm hoping you'll have your purse, but an extra couple of twenties isn't a bad idea. If the power grid goes down, you'll need cash, not credit cards.
- **Flashlight:** It might be dark outside or the power may go out.
- **Water bottle:** Fill it when it makes sense. For example, let's say you have your Get Home Bag and you're staying in a hotel. You might fill the water bottle before you go to bed in case you have to grab the bag and run out during the night.
- **Lightweight rain jacket**
- **Cell phone cable and power bank**
- **Couple of meal replacement bars**
- **N95 mask:** I wouldn't have thought of this before COVID-19, but I sure think of it now. Not only for viruses, but terrorist attacks, dust from explosions, smoke from fires— who knows? It's small, but powerful.

If you work in a dangerous area, you might feel you need a weapon of some sort such as pepper spray. If you wear dressy clothes to work, you might toss in a pair of jeans.

If you work in a big office building and getting to your vehicle is difficult or you take public transportation, stash an extra bag with these items at your desk. If it's easy to get to your vehicle, the bag there is probably all you need. If you travel frequently, have these items in your roller bag or in a backpack and keep them with you. Having a pair of running shoes on 9/11 would have gotten you out of the tower faster. Why not keep a pair handy?

- 20 -

ADDITIONAL TRAVEL TIPS

New environments can present new risks. If you are traveling for pleasure the risks may be different than if you are traveling for business. If my flight gets delayed on a vacation, I won't love it, but it won't upset me as much as a delayed business flight. International travel differs from domestic. Habits we fall into in our daily routines may increase our vulnerability in public spaces.

Travel and Technology

Be careful with public Wi-Fi. Disable auto-connect while traveling. Public Wi-Fi in airports, hotel lobbies, and similar spaces is often targeted by hackers. This will also help your battery last longer. There can be a similarly named decoy Wi-Fi network alongside the legit network. You might see the Hilton network, the Hilton Guest network, and the Hilton2 network. One could be fake, and by connecting you let the bad guys see everything you do as well as possibly infect your system.

Don't use the USB charging stations in airports and other public areas. Unless you have a special cable that only charges and doesn't have the technology to allow data transfer, someone could use the station to get your info or transfer malware to your device. Weirdos and thieves are everywhere. Carry a portable battery with you or use an electrical outlet.

Be alert. This is another form of situational awareness. Notice who might be looking over your shoulder or listening. If you enter a password or other info and Evil Edward is watching, he may be able to access your account later. Don't leave your electronics unattended—in your car or at your table while you go to the bathroom or at the charging station. Your life is on them—don't give strangers access to it.

Flight Delays

I plan all my travel assuming there will be flight delays. (If you don't fly a lot, feel free to skip this section.) My worst nightmare is missing a speaking engagement because my flight was delayed. Here are my tips for you:

Fly with one airline. Status makes a difference if you can get it. I didn't fully grasp this until I got premium status. Premium flyers have a special number to call, their calls get answered faster, and the airlines work harder to make them happy. Trust me, it's worth it.

Have your airline's customer service on speed dial. When people are lining up at the check-in counter, I am already calling. I typically get rebooked before the first person is finished. I get on the check-in counter line, too, however. It might move fast.

Always plan a backup flight. I always have a plan B and sometimes a plan C. If I have to be somewhere the next day and I book myself on the last flight there, I'm an idiot. I usually want two additional options in case something happens to my original flight. Sometimes this isn't possible, but most of the time it is.

Immediately look for options if there is a problem. Don't delay because everyone else will be looking for options too. If the best option is a rental car, jump on it. When a storm shuts down an airport, rental cars disappear quickly. As soon as trouble appears, I reserve a car. I can always cancel it if the flight makes it out. At the first whiff of trouble, I start putting other options into play. Experienced travelers jump into action while everyone else waits for instructions.

I was booked on the first of three flights from Raleigh to Atlanta. A delay was announced for the first flight. I immediately went to another gate where a flight to Atlanta scheduled to leave before mine was boarding. (I was at the airport so early, I could get on it.) They put me on standby, but I didn't make the final boarding list.

I called my premium help line and got put on standby for the next two flights. My original flight was delayed again. Luckily, I got on the next flight. The original flight wound up being delayed by four hours. I would have missed my Atlanta connection, which would have been a serious problem. By the time people on my original flight started looking for alternate flights, everything was booked. Move fast.

Be nice. When delays happen, we are often upset and angry and stressed. You'll have a better chance of getting help if you are nice. It doesn't always work. Some people are rude no matter how nice you are to them, but for the most part, you get back what you give out.

The more prepared you are, the less stressed you are. Always have a backup plan when the flight is important. If you're flexible, relax. You might even get paid to take a later flight.

Practice situational awareness on board. Your normalcy bias is going to convince you there won't be any problems. I sit in the emergency row and I'm always ready to open the emergency door. On one flight, I wasn't sure how to open it from the instructions on the safety card. I asked a flight attendant, and he said, "Don't worry about it." Seriously? I asked another flight attendant.

If you're not in an exit row, look around for the emergency exits. I always do this and seldom see anyone else looking. Do you want to wait until the panic of a real emergency? She who is the most prepared and calm will win. Most people who die in airplane crashes die because they don't get off the plane—they die from smoke inhalation or fire. They try to get their carryon luggage instead of getting out.

You have to move. Know where the exits are and how to open that door. Also notice if someone is acting weird. It was the airline passengers who noticed how strange the would-be shoe bomber was behaving and alerted the crew.

International Travel

You can be at higher risk when you leave your home country. Before you leave the US, check out the travel advisories on the Department of State website. Depending on where you're traveling, you may need certain vaccines or certain documentation. There may be security or weather alerts.

A money belt is useful to protect your cash from pickpockets (I've encountered pickpockets in Manhattan and Rome). Making extra copies of your passport and other important items (driver's license, credit cards) and keeping these separate from the originals is good practice. Not looking like a rich tourist is wise. In some countries, it's better not to advertise where you are from (consider what it says on your T-shirts; being an American might make you a target in some places) or your religion (tuck religious necklaces inside shirts).

You also need to be extra careful with your cybersecurity. Hackers and unsafe networks are everywhere—some places more than others. You might be traveling to a country where your super expensive phone or laptop makes you a target. There are so many variables here, I can't address them all. Just know you need to take extra steps to prepare for travel abroad.

I often go with tour groups when I travel overseas, my favorite is Rick Steves. Here is a link to some of his tips for travel to Europe: https://www.ricksteves.com/travel-tips/theft-scams.

Travel is one of life's best experiences—don't fear it. Proper preparation will help you be safe and enjoy your adventures.

Pink Prep Principle: Being on vacation doesn't mean letting your guard down.

I want you to feel comfortable traveling whether you are making a grocery run or strolling the streets of London. Practice these safety tips regularly and they will become second nature to you. You won't even have to think about them. Most places are safe and you should visit as many of them as you can. Life is a grand adventure, Pink Prepper, and the world is your runway.

- 21 -

SMALL-SCALE DISASTER PREP

S mall-scale disasters are events that only impact you and your family. They are sudden and unexpected and could result in loss of life. Large-scale disasters happen to a wider area, perhaps your neighborhood (power outage), or state or region (tornadoes and hurricanes, snowstorm of the century, chemical leak, wildfires).

Let's start small and work up.

Falls

Falls are much more likely to impact you than any of the other small-scale disasters (house fire, burglary, home invasion). As we age, we might be one fall away from assisted living. This is a big deal and needs to be on your radar.

Tips to reduce the likelihood of a fall:

- **Exercise.** Focus on exercises or activities that strengthen your legs and improve your balance. Apparently, I need to work on my balance so tai chi is on my list.
- **Fall proof (as much as possible) your home.** Keep items off the stairs. No loose or uneven steps—inside or out. Keep stairs and other tricky areas well lit. Make sure there is no clutter, no stray electric cords, no loose rugs to trip/slip on. Have handrails on stairs. Make sure the tub isn't too slippery and be careful in hotels. (One of my dear friends fell and hit her head in a hotel shower. She is not elderly.) No one thinks they are going to fall—until they do. If you don't want to prepare for yourself, prepare for visitors. You would feel horrible if a visitor to your home fell and hurt themselves.
- **Ditch the heels.** Always have some backup shoes. Heels are beautiful, but they increase your risk of falling. Heels can get caught in cracks in the sidewalk. I gave a speech in a building surrounded by a wooden boardwalk. The wood was so full of cracks and fissures, I could hardly get in the building. Ruined the shoes too.
- **Do not mess around with ice. Period.** Get the right shoes and know when to say no. Tim and I were hiking and the stone path became super slick with ice. He wanted to go on, but I refused. I've got nothing to prove to anyone. I am not going to slip off the side of a mountain in an attempt to seem like a badass. Walking on stone covered in ice makes you a dumbass, not a badass.
- **Pay attention and be careful.** Loose stones and gravel, that's what took me down and they can take you down too.

Cobblestones can trip you up. Tree roots covered with leaves are easy to stumble over. Wet leaves can also be slippery and cause you to fall. I usually trip when I am talking instead of paying attention. This is not only for older people. If you hike, you might fall. Pay attention and wear the right shoes.

On a survival show called *Alone*, one of the participants hiked down a mountain. At the bottom, he was walking over stones near a river (quite flat) when he slipped on the stones and broke his leg. He was quite fit, but the terrain was tricky. We are often overconfident.

- **If the lighting is poor, slow down.** When I was in my thirties, I went on a group trip to Australia. One of the ladies (probably in her early sixties) and I were running across a street one night. There was a median in the road, which I stepped on and over, and kept running. She didn't see it at all—ran right into it, fell and hurt herself quite badly. I felt terrible. It never occurred to me that she couldn't see it. As you get older, your night vision gets worse. So if you're not doing these things for yourself, Pink Prepper, do them to help the rest of us.

Pink Prep Principle: If you fail to plan, you plan to fall.

House Fires

The chances of a house fire are quite low, and they usually happen because someone is doing something stupid. But we all do stupid stuff all the time, so a little preparation can't hurt.

Video/photograph all your belongings. If you don't have homeowner's or renter's insurance, get it now. Then video and photograph all your belongings. You'll need this to prove to the insurance company what you had before it all burned to a crisp. Simply shoot a video of each room and narrate as you go. Make sure you open drawers and go in closets. Store your recordings in the cloud for remote access and keep them on your phone if you have storage space.

Realize how fast fire is. According to the Department of Homeland Security, in less than thirty seconds a small flame can turn into a major fire. I saw this happen. Sitting in my office, I looked out the window and saw small flames. The yard across the way was catching fire! I immediately called 911 while watching a man run around with a garden hose. He was having no impact as the flames grew larger.

Luckily, firefighters arrived quickly and put the fire out. The man had dumped his fire pit ashes (which he thought were out) onto a pile of leaves. Before he could say "Smokey Bear," the fire was raging. Remember, prepper, act. If I had worried about overreacting or him being mad at me for calling the fire department, the whole neighborhood might have gone up in flames.

Don't leave food cooking. Don't leave the kitchen if something is on the stove. Soon you'll probably be able to ask Alexa to watch for a fire, but until then, leave a human nearby who can alert you to trouble. Also keep the stove and oven clean. Sometimes food particles can catch on fire.

Be extra careful with candles. I have made many mistakes with candles over the years, and it's a miracle I haven't immolated myself. I've left the house, forgetting a candle was burning. I've assumed all candles were safe. Candles in metal containers are not safe. When the wick burns down, you can be left with a fire in the can. I had to use an oven mitt to carry mine to a sink to drown out the flames. Don't be me. Make sure there is nothing combustible nearby and be extra careful with candles.

Kim had a small candle burning in the main bathroom during a party. The candle burned down to the metal and ignited the vanity, the hand towels, and then the wall. Happily the smoke alarm went off, and she got a bathroom remodel out of it. But it could have been much more serious and deadly.

Pay attention to the clothes dryer. Clean out the filter every single time. It takes two seconds, make it a habit. Think the clothes dryer isn't a big deal? Vicki left the clothes dryer on while she ran a quick errand. She returned home to find firetrucks with flashing lights in her driveway and firefighters hosing down her home. One cat was rescued; the other wasn't so lucky. What wasn't burned up had melted (including her second car in the garage). Smoke alarms not connected to a monitoring service aren't much help when you're not home.

Ditto for the fireplace. Don't toss ashes haphazardly. Let them cool completely and dispose of them in a metal container or hose them down immediately. Don't dump them on a bunch of dried leaves like my neighbor. If you have a log burning fireplace, get a screen and have fireproof rugs around. I have a vivid childhood memory of a big pop and a quarter-sized piece of wood somehow escaping through our fireplace screen and burning a big hole in a rug. My mom nearly had a heart attack. We got a different screen and a different rug. Be careful.

Toss frayed cables and cords. Don't mess with this stuff. Toss iffy cords. If light switches are hot to the touch or lights flicker, get an electrician to fix them.

Smoking—just don't do it. Save money, protect your health, and don't set your house on fire.

Cooking, smoking, candles, clothes dryers, fireplaces, and space heaters are what typically cause fires. So treat a space heater like the others. Don't leave it running unattended, keep things that could catch on fire well away from it, keep it clean and free of debris.

I know these tips seem like commonsense, but most fires start because we are doing something stupid or being careless. Don't be stupid when it comes to fire. It's faster than you can imagine.

Many years ago, I was helping an army jumpmaster set up a nighttime drop zone. This was before high-speed lighting, so we were setting up fires in metal cans to indicate where the parachutists should land. He was adding gas to one of the cans and suddenly flames leaped up the stream of gas, almost engulfing the gas can as well as his arm. It happened faster than anything I've even seen. He was lucky. He dropped the gas can immediately into some sand and it went out. Whew! Do not mess with fire.

Test and replace smoke alarms. I hate it when the batteries start chirping in these. Especially at three in the morning. There must be a better way than trying to figure out where that damn chirp is coming from. It's recommended to test them regularly. Do it at least once a year—maybe October 1st—before you start lighting fires and setting up holiday trees or candles.

Also have smoke alarms on all levels of your home. We have one in the space under our house and in the attic as well as on the main floors. You're supposed to replace the units themselves every eight to ten years. We're due in my house. Crap.

Have fire extinguishers around the house. Have one near the kitchen and an additional one on each floor if you have multiple stories. If you have fireplaces, have one near each. If you cook out on your back deck all the time, maybe you need one there. You also have to know how to use them. I've never operated a fire extinguisher. Here's the PASS acronym printed on ours and on the National Safety Council's website:

- P: Pull the pin. (They have pins?)
- A: Aim at the base of the fire. (Good point—if you start spraying midflame, you might not get the fire out.)
- S: Squeeze the handle slowly. (Not rapidly because you are in a blind panic?)
- S: Sweep the nozzle side to side. (Again, makes sense, but not sure I'd know to do that.)

I need to practice.

Have a fireproof safe. We have one of these for important documents and other items. This is also where cloud backup comes in handy. Get those photos and documents you don't want to lose in a fire backed up in the cloud.

Drop and crawl. The smoke and toxic fumes are often what kill people, not the fire. If you are sleeping and wake up in a fire and see smoke, drop immediately and crawl to safety.

Have a fire escape plan. If you have kids, have a plan to get them out, or if they are old enough, teach them how to get out themselves. Consider my example of the grown people hearing the hotel alarm and staying in the hotel. Do your kids know what to do if the smoke alarms go off in your home? Do you know what to do?

Not knowing the configuration of your home, I can't advise you, but the Department of Homeland Security makes these recommendations:

- Call 911 first. It takes two seconds and they need to start heading your way ASAP.
- Have two ways to exit every room in case the primary way is blocked. Your second exit might be a window. In which case you need to make sure the window can be opened. If it is sealed shut with paint or has bars on it, well, you're going nowhere. You might also need a collapsible ladder for escape if bedrooms are on an upper floor.
- Emergency ladders aren't expensive. If you have kids, you might need a ladder in their rooms. If you have people who are elderly or have special needs in your home, you need to have a plan for getting them out.
- You also need to have a way to get pets out. Now, you do you, but the chances of a fire are so low, I'm going with the ladder, but not a pet carrier.

Pink Preppers do what it takes to feel confident and prepared. I have replaced all my fire alarms, did a walk-through to look for any random fire hazards, bought a third fire extinguisher (one for each level of my home), and bought a ladder so I can escape from my bedroom. I'm done. If you prefer to take it to the next level and get a pet carrier and do fire drills with your kids, fantastic! If having an emergency ladder is too much, that's fine too. Just have a plan for what you'll do if fire breaks out in your home.

Burglary/Break-in

Overall, your chances of being a victim of a break-in are quite low. But it depends on where you live. In 2019, you had a five and a half times greater chance of being the victim of a burglary if you lived in New Mexico compared to New Hampshire. Look at the crime statistics for your neighborhood (try crimemapping.com). If you live in a dangerous area, this may be a higher priority for you than for other Pink Preppers. But, hey, a few simple precautions can make a difference, so why not make them?

Always lock your doors. ALWAYS. I lock Tim out all the time. He's doing yard work, I forget he's out there and lock the door. It's a habit. I close a door to the outside, I lock it. At night, I do the rounds and check all the doors. It's amazing how often someone (we know who) has left a door unlocked. Seriously? If you don't even lock your doors, how can I help you?

Don't post everything on social media. "Whee, we're going to the Caribbean for a week! Look at us! Here we are in the restaurant! Hate to head home today." Thanks for the update. The loser you friended because you didn't want to hurt his feelings just robbed you blind.

Vary your routine. If someone were trying to figure out my routine, it would be impossible—I don't have one. Sometimes I walk at 4:00 p.m., sometimes at 6:00 p.m. When I'm not on pandemic lock-down, I speak on some days and not on others. Casing this joint will give you no clear info. Most burglaries happen between 10:00 a.m. and 3:00 p.m. when people are at work. Burglars don't want to hurt you; they want to take your stuff. If possible, come home for lunch occasionally—anything to vary comings and goings at your home.

Don't leave the garage doors open. Yes, Virginia, the garage is a door. This is a constant point of contention at my house. I always lock the door coming in from the garage to the kitchen. Tim loves to leave the garage doors open as well as this entry door. Sometimes he's out there and sometimes he's not. When I lock him out, I say, "Too bad. What if a killer/robber/bad guy comes by?" If the garage is open, the door to the house needs to be locked. Period. (He carries a key now.)

Aesha's daughter came home late from cheerleading practice and left the garage door open. The next morning the family discovered their cars had been ransacked and the garage cabinets were all open. Plenty of stuff was missing. Cameras showed the burglars in their van cruising the deserted neighborhood at 3:00 a.m., but no faces were seen because of masks and hats. She felt violated. She was. Guess what Aesha does every night? Checks all the doors and locks and makes sure the garage door is closed.

Leaving the garage door open showcases all the cool stuff in there. If you leave it open all the time, you might as well post a sign saying, "Here it is. Come and get it." Also birds will build nests in there. Just close the door.

Rose, a cop, never opens her garage door except for a car to enter or leave. She has been to the scene of too many burglaries where people had seen the Harley or the sports car or the high-end bicycle in the garage and came back later to take them. She said offenders often turned out to be ice cream truck drivers, delivery drivers, or landscapers and other service people who saw someone else's toys and wanted them.

Don't let normalcy bias blind you. I left the house one day and was certain I closed the garage door behind me. Certain. When I came home, it was up. The door to the kitchen was unlocked. My lizard brain was tingling. But did I call 911? Did I even call Tim before entering? No. I wandered in and finally found him out in his workshop (house wide open). But if bad guys had come in, I would have been clueless human prey. I should have at least called Tim before entering. (I was that person in the horror movie you can't believe is stupid enough to go in the spooky house.)

Get a dog. Only if you seriously want and can afford one, but a dog will deter most burglars. Why would a criminal bother with a barking, growling dog if he could simply go to the house next door? And small ones are more of a deterrent than big ones because they are so yappy. However, if the burglar knows you are in the Caribbean because of your Facebook posts and Fifi is at the pet spa, well, what good was a dog then?

Reinforce weak spots. Case the joint yourself. Where would you break in if you were a bad guy? When I lived in a townhome, the sliding glass door on the lowest level was my most vulnerable point. I added a burglar bar for extra security. I also had a burglar alarm, but I set it off more than any burglar ever did.

How are the locks on your doors? Windows? Consider adding motion-activated lights—especially if you have dark areas around your home where someone could hide. There might be shrubs you need to trim. Don't help the bad guys.

Get to know your neighbors. If you know your neighbors, they can keep an eye on your place when you're away. They can also pick up your mail or move your trash cans back when you're not there to do it.

Do not open the door for strangers. If you get as many deliveries as I do, you know your UPS delivery driver. But any weirdo could walk by, scoop up a package, and ring your doorbell pretending to be a legit delivery person. Don't open the door if you're alone. They can leave the package. Trust your gut, Pink Prepper, but always err on the side of caution. If a predator gets in your house while you're home, bad, bad things will happen. They aren't trying to get your stuff; they are trying to get you.

Install security cameras. Again, all this depends on the risk. If you travel a lot, they might be worth it. We were able to see how little time our dog sitter spent with our dogs. You can even get fake cameras and signs to place in key areas.

To summarize, fortify your home to the point it makes sense based on crime rates and your comfort level. Consider getting a dog. And don't post about your vacations, expensive purchases, and luxury toys on social media. You might want to subscribe to crime alerts in your area—try spotcrime.com. I also subscribe to the security alerts from Nextdoor.com (you may have this for your neighborhood). Burglars don't want to get caught, so implement a couple of these ideas, then go on and enjoy your life.

Home Invasion

Even more rare than burglary, home invasion is when someone enters your home when it is occupied. Often their intent is to hurt the people in it. This is why you always keep those doors locked. Most of the recommendations to prevent burglary also help prevent home invasion.

The best thing to do if someone comes into your house is to get out (which is why I like the idea of the fire escape ladder). If someone comes into the house when I'm home alone (my dogs are going to go nuts), I plan to get the hell out the window. Move. Get away.

Have your car's key fob on your bedside table. Hear some lunatic messing with your front/back door? Set off the car alarm before you bolt. The noise might be enough to scare him off and maybe alert the neighbors.

You can plan for defending your home by considering the Five Ds of Perimeter Defense.

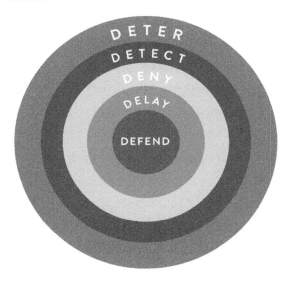

The 5 Ds of Perimeter Defense used with permission from Monty Edge.

Deter is everything you do to make your home a hard target (meaning it seems difficult to gain access to). We want the bad guys to pass on by. This could be anything from barred windows to gates to alarm company signs. It could be lights on a timer or people coming and going at irregular times, closed garage doors, or fencing. Just seeing these things is enough to stop some would-be criminals.

The next ring, **detect**, means being aware the bad guys are there. This could be security cameras, dogs, motion-activated lights, and jingle bells on exterior doors. These can also help serve as deterrents.

Deny is anything you can do to keep the bad guys out once they've decided to try to get in. Barred windows, security locks, thorny bushes, reinforced glass all could come into play here. Our hope is the bad guys won't be able to get in.

These also help with **delay** by slowing the bad guys down long enough for you to call for help (or to prepare to defend). Delay might be extra locks, a safe for valuables, locked bedroom doors—anything that slows them down once they have decided to get in.

Finally there is **defend**. Hopefully, you'll never get to this ring because you've done such a thorough job with all the others. Pink Preppers want to win fights by avoiding them. If you want to prepare for defend, you might want to purchase a gun. If you go that route, get training and practice. Having a gun is a tremendous responsibility, and I know you will not take it lightly.

But let's keep this real. Pink Prepper, we are not badasses. Violence is fast and ugly, and we need to stay as far away from it as we can get. Do you know what we're most likely to do? Freeze. I know—you are an Amazon warrior and that will never happen to you.

Well, I got up one night to go to the bathroom. As I came out of the lit bathroom, I saw a dark, human-shaped figure inside the front door. I froze in terror. I emitted a slight, "Eep." That was it. I couldn't even get a scream out to alert my beloved sleeping down the hall. Luckily, the shape was actually him. He had gotten up while I was in the bathroom to get a drink. So, yeah, you might not break out those ninja moves you think you have. But if you have a plan and practice it in your head, your chances of not freezing are a lot better.

Bottom line—the chance of a home invasion is remote, but if someone comes into your house when you are there, it is a bad, bad thing. Have an escape plan. If you opt for fight rather than flight, train accordingly. The best thing to do is keep that bad man out, but have a plan for what you will do if he gets in.

LARGE-SCALE DISASTER PREP

L arge-scale events impact many people and are what we typically consider disasters. In general, they are unlikely to happen, but the likelihood varies depending on where you live.

The Department of Homeland Security has a *Threat and Hazard Identification and Risk Assessment and Stakeholders Preparedness Review* guide you can download. It is designed to take community leaders through a process like what we're doing. First, they assess which threats and hazards are most likely to happen. Then they assess the potential impact. That helps them prioritize which threats and hazards to plan for.

For example, a beach community in North Carolina would place hurricane preparation well above volcanic eruption preparation. A cyber attack may be equally likely, but not as devastating as a hurricane. Here is table 1 from that publication. It may cause you to consider additional threats you want to prepare for:

Table 1: Example threats and hazards by category

NATURAL	TECHNOLOGICAL	HUMAN-CAUSED
Avalanche	Dam failure	Active shooter incident
Drought	Hazardous materials release	Armed assault
Earthquake	Industrial accident	Biological attack
Epidemic	Levee failure	Chemical attack
Flood	Mine accident	Cyber-attack against data
Hurricane/Typhoon	Pipeline explosion	Cyber-attack against infrastructure
Space weather	Radiological release	Explosive attack
Tornado	Train derailment	Improvised nuclear attack
Tsunami	Transportation accident	Nuclear terrorism attack
Volcanic eruption	Urban conflagration	Radiological attack
Winter storm	Utility disruption	

From the Department of Homeland Security's *Threat and Hazard Identification and Risk Assessment and Stakeholders Preparedness Review*

Before you disregard this section, realize that (according to the Hazards and Vulnerability Research Institute) about 91 percent of Americans live in locations with a moderate to high risk of earthquakes, volcanoes, tornadoes, wildfires, hurricanes, flooding, high-wind damage, or terrorism. This means you, Pink Prepper.

FEMA (Federal Emergency Management Agency) is part of the US Department of Homeland Security and their ready.gov website has a ton of information. Their *Guide to Citizen Preparedness 2020* has the same three steps we cover here: (1) know your risks, (2) make a plan, and (3) take action. They agree it is not *if* you will face challenges, it is *when*. And the government admits it will not be able to help everyone immediately. FEMA doesn't put it quite like this, but for at least a while, you will be on your own.

The best strategy of all—avoidance. We should consider the risks before we move to a new area. We shouldn't buy a home in a flood zone or on a fault line. The oceans are rising, yet people are still buying homes near them. I'm not saying you should move (well, maybe some of you should move), I'm encouraging you to do your homework before your next move.

The disasters addressed here have the widest applicability (more Pink Preppers will experience power outages than avalanches). With each disaster, you have options. You can bug out or shelter at home. Which option you choose depends on many factors, but you should be ready for both.

Power Outage

These often accompany disasters, but can happen with severe weather, damage to transformers, excessive usage, wind, ice, and other random events. The US has an aging power grid, so we should all be prepared for these. According to the US Energy Information Administration, in 2019, US customers experienced an average of 3.2 hours of interruptions during major events and 1.5 hours of interruptions without major events, or nearly 5 hours total. You can see the details for your state here: https://www.eia.gov/todayinenergy/detail.php?id=45796.

Some states have many more outages than others. Maine and West Virginia topped the list in 2019. Maine topped the list due to weather, and West Virginia, well, West Virginia could use some infrastructure improvement. (I'm sure Texas will move up the list in 2021.)

Emergency guides suggest you prepare for three days without power.

If you live in an area with serious winter storms, you might decide to prepare for a week or more. Consider these steps:

Get a generator. We did this right before a three-day outage. Bad winter storms were predicted, and our area is prone to outages anyway. It was the best money we ever spent. We got a portable one, and it was enough to allow us to run our freezer and fridge, charge electronics, and watch TV. If I lived where it took longer for repair crews to get out or power outages were more frequent, I'd consider a whole house generator. That's a major expense, but it might be worth it for you.

Have backup batteries for electronics or medical devices. Since I now give virtual programs, I can't lose power in the middle of a keynote. I have backup batteries on my computer and my router. They won't power them for long, but they buy time to complete a keynote or save what I'm working on. We also have power surges, and the backup battery keeps me rolling without a hitch. If you have medical devices requiring electricity or medicines that need refrigeration, you need a plan for those.

Have lots of alternative light sources and batteries. Get several flash-lights and have them throughout the house. I have one in my bedside table, in the kitchen, the garage and under the house. Be extra careful with candles. If you have pets or children that might knock them over, don't use them. We also have several battery-operated lanterns, which are my favorite. They throw off tons of light, are easy to transport, and seem homier than a flashlight.

Charge backup cell phone batteries. I have several and whenever a storm is coming, I start charging them up. I also like to have an extra charged one with me when I travel. (Saves you from those questionable airport charging stations.)

Gas up your car. Keep a quarter tank at all times, but fill up if bad weather is coming. If the power goes out or there are other problems, you may have to evacuate. Gas stations may be closed or out of gas. Also get gas for your generator. When hurricanes hit South Carolina, gas stations ran out of gas. It was disconcerting, to say the least.

Get a NOAA radio. It gives automated twenty-four-hour all-hazards updates from a nationwide network of radio stations. Messages include weather events, technological incidents like chemical spills, AMBER alerts, and national emergencies. This is helpful to keep an eye (or an ear) on the weather when it gets bad. I got one on Amazon for $35. The one I have can be charged from the wall, can take batteries, has a solar panel, and a hand crank. It also has a flashlight and an emergency alarm feature. It's small so is easy to put in a Bug-Out Bag. You will also get emergency alerts on most cell phones as long as they are charged. The alerts will come in the form of a text with a special tone.

A WATCH means something is possible (be aware). A WARNING means it's already happening or is very likely to happen (take action).

Download your electric company's app. You can get updates (including when they expect power to be restored) and can let the power company know there's an outage in your area. Never assume they already know—someone has to be the first to notify them. Everyone assumes someone else will do it. You be the doer.

Download the FEMA app. You can receive emergency notifications for up to five locations. Maybe you want to keep an eye on the city where your daughter goes to college or where your parents live. Also check to see if your municipality has an app or an alert system you can sign up for. The American Red Cross has an app. The more notice you have that something is heading your way, the more prepared you can be. The Red Cross also has a first aid app and a pet emergency app.

Use Nextdoor and social media. Nextdoor is like Facebook for your neighborhood. I find it helpful during power outages and storms. Neighbors can check to see what others have heard, if everyone has lost power, if driving conditions are bad, and which stores have toilet paper. Your place of work or your children's school may also have emergency communication systems set up. Check on all available and use whatever options work for you.

Texting is your friend. During a real disaster, cell phone lines can get overloaded. Text messages can often get through when calls can't.

Put bottles of water in your freezer now. When frozen, they will help keep the food colder longer if the power goes out. You can also transfer some frozen bottles to your refrigerator if needed. And finally, you can use them for drinking water. If the power does go out, keep freezer and refrigerator doors closed as much as possible.

Assemble an emergency kit. During a power outage, I'm assuming you are staying at home, at least initially. Most of us don't head for the hills if the power goes out. However, if it is the middle of summer with 100-plus–degree temperatures, I might relocate to a hotel with air conditioning (and a spa).

If you plan to ride out a storm or some other disaster at home, you need an emergency kit. You know the one—the kit everyone tells us to assemble, but we never do. If we did, we'd all have had toilet paper, masks, and hand sanitizer when COVID-19 hit. Time to get real, Pink Prepper. Here's what you need:

- Put aside a big pack of toilet paper (or two).
- Ditto for paper towels and hand sanitizer.
- Two or more cases of bottled water. You need one gallon per person per day for at least three days for drinking and sanitation. This is why people often fill up bathtubs with water during power outages. You can use that water to flush toilets, wash dishes, and, if purified, drink. (I have my LifeStraw ready.) What happens to your water during a power outage depends on where you live, but why take a chance? Store some bottled water.
- Food. Most of us probably have enough food on hand for three days. But there's no power, so make sure you have a manual can opener for canned goods. During COVID-19 canned fruits and veggies were bought up quickly and supply chains had problems. Some store shelves were empty for a while. We've added lots of canned goods to our pantry just in case. Canned items last a long time and so does my favorite, peanut butter. Have some extra in case SHTF.
- Masks. Extra N95 masks should be a home staple now.
- Plastic sheeting and duct tape. If there's a nuclear event or a chemical spill, you may need to seal the areas around your windows, doors, and air vents. You may be rolling your eyes, but this only costs a few dollars. And there are some

bad actors in the world—I'd rather be safe than sorry. If you live in an area prone to storms, you may need to have extra plywood on hand to board up windows or tarps for leaky roofs.

- Plain household bleach. Can be used as a disinfectant and, if needed, to treat water (8 drops of regular household bleach per gallon of water). But bleach doesn't last forever. If you keep extra on hand, you'll have to replace it every six months.
- Paper plates and cups and plastic utensils.

Most of the other items you might want, I'm assuming you already have. First aid supplies, garbage bags, chocolate. Don't forget your pets! They'll need food and water too. The key here is that if SHTF, it will be extremely hard to get these things. The COVID-19 situation began almost a year ago, and it's still hard to get certain items in some areas. Have the items here on hand and you'll be prepared for the next crisis.

You may also want to have an emergency kit at work (could be your Get Home Bag) since you don't know where you'll be when the power goes out if there's a big storm. Have a change of clothes (if nothing else, shoes you can run in), backups of any medicines you need, some extra food (jars of peanut butter everywhere). You might even want a flashlight. Include anything you might need/want if stuck at work for a few days. Give it some thought now, put a few items together and, presto, you're done.

Bug-Out Bag (aka Emergency Evacuation Kit)

Some disasters require you to evacuate. If you live on the coast and the authorities tell you to evacuate because a huge hurricane is coming, evacuate. If my FEMA app tells me there is an accident at the nuclear plant, I'm heading for the hills. You must have some form of alert activated so you get as much warning as possible.

When you get the warning, don't think, "Well, I'll be okay. I'll wait and see what happens." In 2011 a tornado in Joplin, Missouri, killed 161 people, and 78 percent of the population received notice a tornado was coming, but only 17 percent acted. All your preps are useless if you don't act when the time comes.

The Bug-Out Bag is something traditional preppers spend a lot of time debating. Articles and books and blog posts have been written about what this bag should contain. Tim has spent a fortune on items in his bag. I'm not going there. If you want to become a disaster ninja and assemble a bag that will help you get through an alien invasion or TEOTWAWKI, you go, girl.

I've listed the items you might want to assemble to get you out of your home and to safety if it took a couple of days. If I can't get someplace safe in a couple of days with everything in this bag, well, there's been an utter breakdown of society, chocolate factories are closed, and I'm not sure I'll want to go on. But if you want to live in a chocolateless world, I've given you resources in the bonus section.

The Bug-Out Bag is a bag you could grab if you had to "bug out" or leave your house quickly due to an emergency. I don't see an emergency in which I will not be driving my car, at least part of the way. If you don't have a car, you'll have to adjust this plan accordingly.

What will you need to survive three days?

- Water
- Food
- Shelter

I'm going to horrify every traditional prepper with this advice. But I told you all in the beginning, this is practical prep. If a wildfire is heading this way, I'll get some warning. I'll jump in my car and head out if that's what I'm told to do. I will grab my purse and drive to a hotel. I'm not setting up a tent and surviving in the wilderness. The chance of something happening that requires me to evacuate without my car is so small, I'm not worrying about it. Now, if you live in a high rise in Manhattan and rely on public transportation, your situation is different. You need a more serious exit strategy.

In case you are thinking, "I'll never need to leave my home," let me give you some reasons you might have to leave:

- Social unrest
- House fire
- Weather event
- Hazardous material or nuclear event
- Wildfire
- Dam collapse or other flooding
- The FBI finally catches up with you

For most of the events I've listed, if you leave quickly enough, you can get out and get to a hotel outside the danger zone. (This is why you have to have money, Pink Prepper.) If you wait too long or don't have money for a hotel or friends to stay with, you are going to the government shelter. We want to avoid that if possible, for two reasons: (1) We are Pink Preppers—we do not want to be a burden to others in this time of crisis. We are prepared and can take care of ourselves and our families; and (2) Bad things can happen in overcrowded, understaffed shelters.

Here's my plan. We store bottled water in the garage. I can grab a case and throw it in my car. I also have a relatively small bag of dog food I could toss in as well. The dog bowls and leashes are right there—bam, they are in. I already have the bag we put together earlier in my car. I throw in a box of granola bars and protein bars (also near the garage) and my laptop—I'm outta here. We can live in the car long enough for me to get someplace out of the disaster zone.

But, Denise, you say, "What about a first aid kit?" What the hell am I gonna do with a first aid kit? I'm not planning on causing myself any injuries. And if I do get hurt badly enough to need medical attention, I'm not going to be able to fix myself with a first aid kit. But you do you. If you have kids and/or know first aid, you should already have this in your car in the bag we put together earlier. But you can add it to this bag if you like.

You do need to pack up your prescriptions and any over-the-counter meds you want (probably won't hurt to have some Aleve and Pepto/Tums).

The only other thing you should add to this list is important documents. What would you need to rebuild if your house burned down? Chances are you'll have ID, credit cards, and insurance cards in your purse. You might also want to grab your passport, extra cash, your social security card, and your list of passwords (if not stored in another way). If you have other important documents scanned and saved on a zip drive or uploaded to the cloud, you're ready. If you feel better with hard copies, get a waterproof, fireproof box for them and grab it if you bug out.

To help you remember, FEMA talks about the five Ps of evacuation:

- People (includes pets, livestock—anything that depends on you to live)
- Prescriptions (also medical equipment if needed)
- Papers (important documents)
- Personal needs (clothes, food, water, hygiene items)

- Priceless items (irreplaceable pictures, mementos, valuables). Personally, I think this is a distraction you don't need. Unless you have tons of time, just get out. Nothing is as priceless as your life.

This list is not bad if it helps you remember. But better is to have your Bug-Out Bag ready. Do you want to attempt to gather important documents as a hurricane bears down on you? Put it together now, and you can quickly escape from anything that comes your way.

Barbara and Alan live on the Gulf of Mexico side of Florida. Evacuating for impending hurricanes has become almost an annual event for them. Fortunately, they have friends who live inland about forty miles where they have a standing invitation to shelter.

Well before hurricane season, they assemble what goes into the car (including a file of important papers with passports and their daily medicines). Family photo albums are in high cupboards in case the condo floods. They figure they can buy clothes or necessities at a Walmart near their friends' home. So they know they can bug out in minutes and beat the traffic. So far they haven't come home to a waterlogged place. So far.

Hazardous Materials/Nuclear Incident

If you live near a highway where trucks might be transporting dangerous materials, or a nuclear plant like me, or a manufacturing plant that deals with hazardous chemicals, or a mainline for cross-country train traffic, there could be an accident. You might be out driving and a truck with those hazardous waste emblems flips over. (Wondering what those emblems look like? The free ERG 2020 app developed by the Department of Transportation has them all.)

You need to get away as fast as possible, not letting any of the air get in your vehicle. Turn the heat and the AC off and keep the windows and vents closed. If you are outside, stay uphill, upstream, and upwind if possible and get indoors as quickly as you can. Get your kids and pets inside with you. And if you have some of those N95 masks, here we go again. Put them on.

If you are at home and told to shelter in place, this is where that plastic sheeting and duct tape come into play. Seal any cracks and openings. Close fireplace dampers. Turn off the AC. Close interior doors. If you can find a room with no windows, shelter there with the door closed and cracks under the door blocked. For how long? Twenty-four hours. This is from the CDC's website:

> A nuclear power plant accident, a nuclear explosion or a dirty bomb are examples of radiation emergencies. If something like this happens, you may be asked to get inside a building and take shelter for a period of time instead of leaving. The walls of your home can block much of the harmful radiation. Because radioactive materials become weaker over time, staying inside for at least twenty-four hours can protect you and your family until it is safe to leave the area.

The Department of Homeland Security gives similar instruction for hazardous materials incidents (why I've grouped them together here, although obviously the duration and impact of each can vary widely).

You're probably thinking, "What? Shelter in one room for twenty-four hours? Are you kidding me?" I bet you'd figure it out if there was radiation outside! But it does lead us to discuss a safe room.

For some SHTF situations (a nuclear or hazardous materials event, a tornado or hurricane) you need a room in your house to retreat to. Everyone reading this book is in a different situation, but most of us have a room with no windows. At our house, we have one small bathroom that would work, we also have a workshop space under our house.

Much of prepping is simply considering what you'll do if something happens. Then if it does, you can act instead of standing there wondering what to do while being zapped with radiation. Assess the SHTF situations most likely to happen to you and plan accordingly.

When I lived in Oklahoma, my in-laws had a fully stocked storm shelter under their sunroom. I had no idea it was even there until a tornado came, and we all went down. The house was fine, but they had frequent serious storms, so it was a worthwhile investment for them.

Plan for where you live and what your risk is and do what you can afford to feel safe. You are *definitely* going to retire someday. You *might* be in a tornado. Do not build a storm shelter at the expense of your retirement. But do have a plan for a major storm. Plans are free, but most people don't make them.

For most people, this is all you need for a safe room:

- A room all family members (and pets) can fit in that has no windows.
- A bathroom is nice for obvious reasons (water and a toilet).
- Keep in this room or in an easily grabbed bag, your phone and charger, NOAA radio, food—whatever you'd need to stay in that room for up to twenty-four hours.
- Plastic sheeting and duct tape.

If the only thing you are worried about is a bad storm, all you need to do is to pick the room and make sure your family knows to go there and under what circumstances. Preparation now could make all the difference later.

If there is a nuclear plant near you, do your homework. The nuclear plant near me has a map on its website that shows the danger zone, and we are right on the edge. I want to get the hell away from that thing as quickly as possible if there's an incident, but I may have to shelter in place. There is also an emergency preparedness guide on the plant's website:

Cover of the Harris Nuclear Plant's Preparedness Guide

Check the website of any facility near you, read the information, craft a plan, get some potassium iodide (on Amazon for next to nothing), and move on.

Dam Collapse/Flooding/Storms/Wildfire

Check out the National Inventory of Dams website maintained by the US Army Corps of Engineers. Sign in as General Public and use the Interactive Map & Charts to check out your county and see if you live near one. Chances are good that you do.

I visited Coulee Dam's website and all I could find was the statement that the dam probably wouldn't break, but water could overflow and flooding could occur. There are hundreds of dams in every state, and some are old and in disrepair. It's possible one could break or flood. Unlikely, but possible. But a dam overflowing or breaking is not the only way you could be the victim of flooding.

The Department of Homeland Security's publication "How to Prepare for a Flood," states "Flooding is the most common natural disaster in the United States and can happen anywhere." We had extensive flooding in North Carolina after a hurricane. The storm surge combined with already high rivers to cause devastation far inland. Areas were flooded that had never been flooded before. There can also be flooding after a snowstorm as snow melts and rivers and lakes overflow. Or a flooded dam hundreds of miles upstream from you sends water cascading into swollen rivers where you live.

If you live in a flood zone, you should plan for the possibility of flooding. Definitely consider flood insurance (in some states, it is required). Homeowner's insurance typically does not cover damage due to flooding. Also see what you can do to your home to protect it—waterproofing your basement, elevating or floodproofing electrical systems, and using flood-resistant building supplies below the base flood elevation (BFE). That's the level water is expected to reach if there is a flood. An example would be replacing carpet with tiles.

You don't have to run out and do this anytime soon, but if you plan to redecorate or remodel, keep this in mind. And don't store anything important below the BFE. Just in case.

Before you think, "This won't happen to me" (normalcy bias), the National Weather Service estimates in an average year, the United States has a thousand tornadoes and ten hurricanes. Those storms can drop huge amounts of water. Also as sea levels rise, the impact of hurricanes and flooding is greater. Rainfall amounts are also increasing globally. Areas that haven't flooded before, could flood now.

How to prepare:

Keep gutters and downspouts clear. You should do this all the time—water can do serious damage to your home over time. We bought a house that had been vacant for years. The gutters were packed with debris. One of the window frames was damaged inside and out because water hit it over and over. If the gutters had been cleared, water would have never touched the frame. Don't let laziness destroy your biggest investment. Consider gutter guards. Keeping the gutters clear also helps with fire prevention.

Install flood vents. If you live in an area prone to flooding, flood vents allow water to flow through and drain out rather than filling your crawl space or garage.

Stockpile sandbags. If you live in an area prone to flooding, you might want to have some sandbags or other building material on hand. Anything you can do to keep water from entering your home helps.

While we're talking about preparing your home in case of a flood, let's talk about high winds. If you live in an area prone to hurricanes, storm shutters or hurricane straps on roofs (I didn't even know there was such a thing) can lessen the damage.

We all learned a new word, *derecho*, when high winds swept down the Plains states in 2020 and knocked over crops and trees. It's hard to plan for such an unusual and rare event that's not seasonal. But battening down lawn furniture is always prudent and taking down old and dying trees may prevent one from dropping through your roof.

Pay attention to alerts so you can evacuate if needed. They include flood warnings. The injuries and deaths associated with floods happen because people get trapped in flood water. So if told to evacuate, do it. Why? Because it's beyond selfish to put yourself in harm's way and make first responders risk their lives coming to get you. If someone who truly couldn't get out (poor Mrs. Jones who is eighty-nine) dies because you wanted to stay and protect your big screen TV, shame on you.

Believe me, they don't tell you to evacuate for fun; they tell you to evacuate to save your life and the lives of others. Do it. And better to do it sooner rather than later. Why? If you wait, you might get caught in the traffic of all the people leaving. Or the flood waters might rise so high, you can't get out. Or all the hotels and shelters fill up.

You'll need to have a plan for where you are going. I always have cash and credit cards on hand, and I'll drive as far as I need to get to a hotel. Do you have some friends you can go to or family? Perfect! Make sure you talk about this in advance and don't simply assume. They may not be delighted to see you, your eight children, and forty-three parakeets. Most public shelters don't let you have pets, so plan for your fur babies too.

Follow the route you are directed to take. If there are barricades, don't drive around them. They are set up for a reason—maybe a bridge is out. Don't drive, walk, or swim through flood waters. Just six inches of moving water can knock you down and one foot of moving water can sweep your car away.

Flood water is nasty, prepper. Stay out of it if you can. And you know what they say, "Turn around, don't drown." Stupid, but memorable. (Most people who die in hurricanes die of drowning—get away from the water during these events. Storm surge can happen fast and far inland.)

All the tips that follow are to consider if you have time. Don't get trapped because you're trying to clear the gutters.

If leaving due to storms/flooding—

- Move valuables to higher floors.
- Roll up rugs and stand them vertically or they will soak up water and be ruined.
- Turn off gas, water, and electricity if you can do so safely.
- Put sandbags around doors—don't forget the garage door.
- Make sure all gutters and drains are clear.

If there are high winds, also—

- Secure outdoor objects that could become airborne—lawn furniture, trash cans, toys, grills, bird feeders. If you can't bring something inside (like a grill), anchor it in some way.
- If you don't have hurricane shutters, nail plywood over windows. Tape placed across windows doesn't work (although I see it all the time). The plywood needs to be at least a half-inch thick and suitable for outdoor use. (Would be smart to have plywood on hand before you need it if you live in a danger zone.)

- Close all interior doors. If a window does break, and the house becomes depressurized, the doors will help support the roof. (Who knew?)

If leaving due to wildfires—

- In the US, wildfires are most frequent in the West, but all wooded, brush-filled, and grassy areas are vulnerable. (One neighbor and some fire pit ashes ...)
- Consider wearing N95 masks to protect you from dust and smoke.
- Don't lock the windows and doors. The firefighters may need to get in.
- If you have a propane tank system, turn off the valves.
- Wet down your roof (if combustible).
- Close all the doors and windows inside your home to prevent drafts.
- Leave fire tools (shovels, hoes, and hoses) outside in front of the house for firefighters to use.
- Leave garden hoses connected.
- Move anything that's combustible away from the house— pool umbrellas, tarps, firewood.
- Move combustible furniture toward the center of the room away from windows and sliding glass doors.

If you are NOT evacuating, and a big storm is coming—

- Turn that NOAA radio on.
- Get your emergency kit (power may go out).

- Do everything already mentioned to protect the house.
- Fuel your car, just in case. Also get gas for your generator.
- Store drinking water in clean bathtubs, sinks, and jugs in case the local water supply becomes contaminated or you need to flush the toilet. If this is a concern for you, the EPA has a detailed discussion of emergency drinking water on its website.
- Get to your safe room.

Learn about lightning. We've all seen those blockheads who continue to swim when a thunderstorm is clearly upon them. But did you know, in many years, lightning kills more people than any other kind of weather? One hundred lightning strikes hit the earth every second.

According to the National Weather Service, your odds of being struck in your lifetime are one in 15,300 (as a comparison, your odds of being in a shark attack are one in 11.5 million). The likelihood varies widely by state with Texas and Florida leading the way. Lightning mostly kills men due to a combination of factors—hobbies (fishing, outdoor sports), occupation (construction), and stubbornness (they are less likely to want to cancel golf plans due to a little thunder).

Remember this cheesy phrase, "When lighting roars, go indoors." Not under cover—you need four walls and a roof. A gazebo is no good. A car with the windows rolled up is good. A golf cart is not. Stay away from water, metal, and electronics even if inside. (Cell phones and cordless phones are okay to use.)

If outside, get inside. Don't lie on the ground. Lightning can be deadly over 100 feet away from where it strikes. Don't stand under a tall tree. If you can hear thunder, go inside. Wait at least thirty minutes after the last clap before going back out. And lightning can strike twice (it hits the

Empire State Building about 100 times a year). Pink Preppers are okay here but tell the men in your life if thunder roars, go indoors (eye roll emoji). And use surge protectors for your computers and other expensive electronics.

Other Disasters

If you live in an area prone to earthquakes, the biggest danger is something falling on you like the bookcase next to your desk. Secure shelves to walls and take other precautions. Know that standing in a doorway is not the best response. Better to drop, cover your head, and hold on. Get under a piece of sturdy furniture (desk or table) if you can.

Landslides, volcanoes, tsunamis—get the hell out of there! If you live in an area that might have such an occurrence, move someplace else. Seriously, learn the warning signs, sign up for alerts, and be prepared to make a run for it. Same is true for any giant destructive force that is bearing down on you—your mother-in-law, the IRS . . . you get it.

All the tips—emergency supplies, Bug-Out Bag—still apply. Don't take chances. You absolutely will lose in a battle with the forces of nature in the form of mud, volcanic eruptions, ash, and wind and water. I encourage you to research any disasters that are possibilities for your area and prepare accordingly.

- 23 -

WAR/TERRORISM/ACTIVE SHOOTER

If we go to war, you should get some advance notice. If a nuclear weapon is heading this way, well, short of an underground bunker, there is not much we can do to prepare (unless you are far away from the impact zone and do what was recommended to protect yourself from the fallout).

As far as acts of terrorism or an active shooter, your best preparation is situational awareness. People who are up to no good tend to act oddly. If you see something that causes you concern, get away. The sooner you do, the better. Tell authorities if appropriate (if you see something, say something).

Be aware of possible clues. Disaffected kids posting scary pics on social media is a clue. Maybe you need to have a talk with your children about indicators to look for and what to do. Watch the YouTube video *Evan/Sandy Hook Promise* (protect kids from gun violence). Clues are often there, but our normalcy bias blinds us.

If there is an active shooter, here's what to do: RUN! Always choose this response first. Get as far away as fast as you can. Know where the exits are in places you frequent. If other people don't want to go, leave them. Some people who aren't Pink Preppers will be stunned by their normalcy bias. Maybe your running will snap them out of it. Don't stop and gather your belongings or take video or photos of the shooter. Get out.

I've watched several videos of active shooter incidents, and, unfortunately, many people automatically drop to the floor and cover their heads. The shooter just shoots them. MOVE! Run away—a moving target is extremely hard to hit.

HIDE! This is your next option. If you are hiding, silence your cell phone—don't even leave it on vibrate. Block or lock doors, turn off lights, close blinds. Wherever you are, try to put something solid between yourself and the attacker (block or brick walls are your best bet). Bullets go through sheet rock and wood.

FIGHT! This is your last option and only do it if your life is in immediate danger. You must give this your full commitment. It is the shooter or you. During the Pulse nightclub shooting in Orlando, several people ran into a restroom to hide. When the shooter came in, he shot many of them. If they had rushed him when the door opened, they might have overtaken him and survived. (I am not in any way suggesting they were at fault. I only use this as an example of a last resort option.)

Many in the club that night thought the shots were fireworks. After other shootings, people said they thought the shots were part of the show or the movie. Normalcy bias is not your friend. If there is even a remote chance a noise is gunfire—run away.

If you are at any event (peaceful protest, crowded bar, football game) and there's violence, get away. Usually it starts as a disturbance and people start to look in that direction. Then there can be panic and a huge crush as everyone tries to move away. Here are some tips:

- Know where the exits are and don't hesitate to use them. You may be able to get out before the panic hits.
- Leave if the crowd seems to be getting out of control.
- Wear closed-toe shoes and keep the laces tied to prevent tripping. (No one notices those cute sandals—save your toes.) Littering the stairwells after 9/11 were piles of high heels.
- Avoid standing on or near anything that could collapse (goal posts, balconies filled with people, decks, bleachers).
- Move to the edge of a crowd rather than pushing through it. Walk sideways or diagonally and work your way out.
- Leave early or late to avoid the rush when an event is over.
- Pick a place to meet if your group gets separated. (We got separated at the State Fair—no place to meet, couldn't hear phones, what a disaster.) Set your phone to vibrate as well as ring—anything to get your attention.

Workplace Violence

Here are some indicators a person in your workplace might become violent:
- Increased use of alcohol and/or drugs
- Unexplained increase in absenteeism
- Noticeable decrease in attention to appearance or hygiene
- Depression/withdrawal
- Mood swings
- Resistance and overreaction to changes in policies/procedures
- Repeated violations of company policies
- Noticeably unstable, emotional responses
- Talks of violence or comments about weapons or violent crimes

- Increasing talk of problems at home or severe financial problems

Does this mean someone having personal problems needs to be reported to HR? Absolutely not. Remember the rule of threes. If you see three of these (or three other things that concern you), then act. Say something to someone who can take action, don't just gossip with a coworker. Never ignore your instincts. If your gut says someone is about to lose it, get away.

- 24 -

TRAITS OF THOSE WHO OVERCOME

manda Ripley in *The Unthinkable* writes that during a disaster we all start in the same place and travel through three phases. We begin in **denial**. We think, "This can't be happening." "This can't happen here." "This can't be happening to me." We try to find other explanations—fireworks, not gunshots; kids playing, not screaming; a drill, not a real alarm.

Once we snap out of denial (and the sooner we can snap out of it the better), we move into **deliberation**. We know something is wrong and we're trying to figure out what to do about it. This is where fear can freeze you. But here's to you, Pink Preppers. In their book, *Deadly Force Encounters,* authors Alexis Artwohl and Loren Christensen say, "The actual threat is not nearly as important as the level of preparation. The more prepared you are, the more in control you feel, and the less fear you will experience."

Sums up the work we're doing perfectly. We prepare to lessen our fear and to be able to act. I'll still be scared if I'm in a plane crash, but by knowing how to open the emergency exit, I'm prepared. I know what to do and can move more quickly out of denial, through deliberation to **action**. Knowing what you would do if something happens dramatically increases your chance of survival.

Traits of survivors (not only of disasters but health issues or car accidents as well) include these:

- They are not obese. This isn't to make anyone feel bad. It's difficult to quickly exit a vehicle or run down flights of stairs if you are extremely overweight. All these events are stressful, and the strain on your heart can be tremendous.
- They believe they can influence what happens to them. They also believe they can learn from what happens to them—good or bad.
- They are confident. Often this confidence comes from training and preparation. That's you, Pink Prepper.
- They get through denial and deliberation quickly and act. By reading this book and considering what you would do in a fire, you will move much more quickly to action. Same with practicing situational awareness. You may get out because you took two seconds to determine where the exits were. Everyone else will still be sitting there waiting for someone to tell them what to do.

The National Transportation Safety Board found that passengers who took the time to read the safety information card significantly reduced their risk of injury or death in a plane crash. They knew what to do and could act faster because they were prepared. Going forward, that will be you. A couple of seconds at the beginning of a flight or a glance around a new restaurant for the exit could save your life. Your attention is your greatest tool; your mind, your best weapon.

STEP FIVE IN PINK PREP PLAN–ACT

We have covered a lot of ground together. After reading everything, you may want to review your scores on the Pink Prep Risk Assessment. Maybe you are more (or less) concerned about some risks than you were before. This is your assessment, so change it as needed to reflect your priorities.

You will find that areas overlap, so in prepping for one, you are preparing for others. Being financially prepared for the loss of your partner also helps you prep for health issues (you'll need money to pay for healthcare or replace income if unable to work). Preparing for a health issue helps you better handle a pandemic or a car accident.

This process doesn't have to be expensive and doesn't have to be done all at once. You can pick up an extra jar of peanut butter or can of tuna each time you go to the store. You can download Quicken WillMaker and do your own will. Small actions can have big results.

Once you have your top three (if you have fully prepared for one, you can move down the list), create an action plan to address them. Fill out the following:

My top risk is _____

_____

To prepare, I will—

1. _____

_____

Deadline is _____

2. _____

_____

Deadline is _____

3. _____

_____

Deadline is _____

My second risk is _____

_____

To prepare, I will—

1. _____

_____

Deadline is _____

2. _____

_____

Deadline is _____

3. _____

_____

Deadline is _____

My third risk is _____

_____

To prepare, I will—

1. _____

_____

Deadline is _____

2. _____

_____

Deadline is _____

3. _____

_____

Deadline is _____

I've included deadlines because if you don't set a deadline, your normalcy bias will kick in and you won't act. If it's something that doesn't have a deadline (continuing your diet or exercise program), write *ongoing*. Review this list every January and update it.

Something is heading your way. Working this program will prepare you to meet it. It will also help you enjoy your life more. If you aren't worried about your relationships, health, finances, and safety (because you are Pink Prepped and ready for anything), you can move through life with confidence. And your preparation allows you to help others.

A Final Word to the Pink Prepper

It is my wish for you, not that you will worry all the time, but that you will prepare and then go rock your life.

My emergency fund allowed me to weather the COVID-19 crisis and write this book for you. There are hundreds of thousands of women not so lucky. Thousands of hotel employees, food service workers, and small-business owners who lost everything. You're lucky if you weren't impacted—this time.

Something in the future is barreling toward you right now. Do your future self a favor and prepare. Put on your suit of pink armor now and whatever is coming will bounce right off you. If you wait to don your armor until it slams into you, it will be too late.

Thank you for reading this and for taking the time to prepare. Your preparation not only serves you and your family, it serves others by freeing up government resources to help those truly in need. I hope you'll join me at www.PinkPrep.com to keep in touch and share ideas for staying prepared— and share your preparedness stories too. And spread the word. A prepared woman is a confident, independent woman, and the world needs more of us.

BONUS SECTION

Pink Prepper Risk Assessment

Refer to chapter 7 for the explanation of this tool. You can also find a downloadable copy of this assessment at www.PinkPrep.com.

Possible Risk	Probability	Likelihood from 0 to 5	Impact from 1 to 5	Risk Score C times D	Personal Pink Priority Rank
RELATIONSHIP					
Divorce/break-up	45%				
Death of partner	80% chance of outliving spouse				
Abuse - emotional, physical	25%				
Rape	if age 12 to 34 - 13% if 35 to 64 - 5% 65 and up less than 1%				
Betrayal	20%				
Other family crisis	25 to 100%				
FINANCIAL					
Unexpected financial hardship	100%				
Identity theft	16%				
Cyber attack	23%				
Not enough for retirement	use an online calculator to assess				
HEALTH					
Disability, health issue	see text for guidance				
Arthritis	31% up to age 64, then 69%				
Pandemic	100% (we just don't know when)				

Possible Risk	Probability	Likelihood from 0 to 5	Impact from 1 to 5	Risk Score C times D	Personal Pink Priority Rank
TRAVEL TROUBLES					
Car crash	see text for guidance				
Car trouble	varies with condition of car, etc.				
Crime	depends on location/amt of travel				
Flight delays	20% of all flights delayed				
LOCALIZED DISASTERS					
Falls	50% if you've fallen before, 25% if 65+				
House fire	less than 1% in any given year				
Home break-in	less than 1%				
Home invasion	far less than 1%				
LARGE SCALE DISASTERS					
Power outage	100% at some point				
Natural disaster	depends on where you live				
Hazardous material incident	depends on where you live				
War/terrorism/active shooter	less than 1%				

Nutritional Tool

NUTRIENTS	RECOMMENDED DAILY	EDAMAME	FIBER ONE CEREAL	ALMONDS
Fiber	22g	4.7g	18g	3g
Calcium	1200 mg	59mg	130mg	70mg
Protein	46g	10.59g		6g
Iron	8 mg	2.12mg	3.6mg	1 mg
Magnesium	320 mg		8%*	
Zinc	8 mg		20%*	
Vitamin D	600 IU			
Vitamin A	700 mg			
Potassium	4700 mg	482mg		200mg
Vitamin C	75 mg		10%*	
Vitamin E	15 mg			

*Note - sometimes you will only find percentage of daily requirement on nutrition labels

RECOMMENDED RESOURCES

Books

Self-Defense and Safety

The Gift of Fear: Survival Signals that Protect Us from Violence, Gavin de Becker

Left of Bang: How the Marine Corps' Combat Hunger Program Can Save Your Life, Patrick Van Horne and Jason A. Riley

The New Super Power for Women: Trust Your Intuition, Predict Dangerous Situations, and Defend Yourself from the Unthinkable, Steve Kardian

Spotting Danger Before It Spots You: Build Situational Awareness to Stay Safe, Gary Quesenberry

Stay Safe: Security Secrets for Today's Dangerous World, Greg Shaffer

Survive the Unthinkable: A Total Guide to Women's Self-Protection, Tim Larkin

Disaster Preparedness

Handbook to Practical Disaster Preparedness for the Family, Arthur T. Bradley

Prepper's Instruction Manual: 50 Steps to Prepare for Any Disaster, Arthur T. Bradley

The Provident Prepper, A Common-Sense Guide to Preparing for Emergencies, Kylene Jones and Jonathan Jones

Start Prepping! Get Prepared—For Life: A 10 Step Path to Emergency Preparedness So You Can Survive Any Disaster, Tim Young

The Unthinkable: Who Survives When Disaster Strikes—and Why, Amanda Ripley

Television Show

Surviving Disaster with former Navy SEAL Cade Courtley (2009) has an episode on every disaster you might encounter (available on Amazon Prime Video).

Website

Disaster preparation: www.ready.gov: FEMA's ready.gov has tons of helpful information for disaster preparation. You can find details on a wide variety of specific events as well as a list of publications you can order for free.

ACKNOWLEDGMENTS

I thank my sweetheart, Tim Palmer, for being a prepper and having N95 masks when SHTF during COVID. You've been incredibly supportive during this challenging time and have been my greatest cheerleader. You'll look cute in the Pink Prep Squad uniform.

Kristina Andronica, thank you for being the friend who tells me what I need to hear, not just what I want to hear. I would be in a facility someplace if not for your friendship during the pandemic. You and I have walked the Pink Prep Path together for years, and I could have no better companion on the journey.

Thanks to Kellie Welch and Bobbi Curris for dragging me into virtual presentations and hiring me for the first ones I gave. Not only have you lifted me up, you've done the same for countless military spouses with your leadership and kindness. Knowing you both has been a joy and an honor.

Thanks to Robin Necci and Toby Page of the ABWA Heart of the Piedmont Chapter for hosting the world premier presentation of Pink Prep. Now you all are the Pink Prep Posse. Thanks for your friendship and support over the years.

Thanks to all my clients. It's an act of trust to bring in a speaker, and I'm eternally grateful to everyone who trusted me. Each of you contributed to the emergency fund that allowed me to write this book during the COVID-19 shutdown.

ABOUT THE AUTHOR

Denise Ryan has been speaking professionally for more than twenty years. She is a Certified Speaking Professional, a designation of excellence held by less than 10 percent of professional speakers. She has given over 1,000 presentations and is a certified virtual presenter, certified health coach, and certified financial educator.

She holds an MBA from the University of South Carolina where she graduated Magna Cum Laude with honors from South Carolina College.

She has presented to audiences from four to four thousand and for organizations as varied as Mothers of Multiples and the US Department of Homeland Security. Her clients include Wells Fargo, IBM, the American Business Women's Association, Subway, Blue Cross Blue Shield, and Princeton University. She has one of the highest rates of repeat and referral business in the speaking industry. In short, her audiences love her.

Her favorite audience member quote is this: "I just wanted to let you know how fantastic you were at the Sales Conference in San Diego. I have been in sales and marketing for over twenty-five years and have heard and seen some really good speakers and presenters. I have to say, you were one of the best motivational speakers I have ever heard. Your presentation was excellent, motivating, uplifting, and downright entertaining and let me not forget funny as all get out."

Denise's innovative presentations include these topics:

- Motivation by Chocolate
- How to Communicate with Everyone Who Isn't You
- Staying Motivated No Matter What
- Increasing Your Personal Power for Women
- Pink Prepping—How Women Can Be Prepared for Anything

She was featured on the cover of *Arthritis Today* magazine, showcasing how fitness and attitude can impact recovery from surgery (she has two new hips thanks to her arthritis). She is a volunteer for her local Community Emergency Response Team. She is a former board member of the Association Executives of North Carolina and a recipient of their Patsy B. Smith Award, which recognizes outstanding professionalism and exemplary service to the association community.

Denise lives outside Raleigh, North Carolina, with her beloved, Tim Palmer, and their two dogs Kenda (a solid black German Shepherd) and Banks (a Golden Retriever). She is addicted to true crime, murder mysteries, and all things sweet. She serves on Krispy Kreme's Review Crew and hopes to die by drowning in a vat of donut glaze.

Connect with Denise (and see her in action) at
www.firestarspeaking.com

Made in the USA
Columbia, SC
26 October 2021